THE THREE ROOMS

CHANGE YOUR THOUGHTS,
CHANGE YOUR LIFE

KEVIN MURPHY

RIVER GROVE
BOOKS

Published by River Grove Books
Austin, TX
www.rivergrovebooks.com

Distributed by River Grove Books

Design and composition by Greenleaf Book Group
Cover design by Greenleaf Book Group and Renee Duran

Publisher's Cataloging-in-Publication data is available.

Print ISBN: 978-1-63299-190-4

eBook ISBN: 978-1-63299-191-1

First Edition

To my children, Brendan, Paul, and Rebecca . . .
you are all miraculous.

Contents

FOREWORD

KEVIN MURPHY AND I FIRST MET IN THE FALL OF 1972. HE WAS
a twelve-year-old seventh grade student and I was a twenty-two-
year-old rookie social studies teacher. For the next six years, I
served as his wrestling and lacrosse coach at Lynbrook High
School on Long Island. Murph became one of our finest champions, and we developed a strong bond that only increased after
his graduation.

There was definitely something about Murph that made him
different from the other kids, but I couldn't put my finger on it
then. A light seemed to shine from him that attracted me but
which I could not identify. I believe now that I was looking at
the early development of a young mystic then. Nevertheless, at
that time I was in no state of mind to recognize him as such.
He certainly had little understanding of the spiritual gifts he
was receiving.

Later, at the ages of forty-three and thirty-three respectively, we simultaneously became single dads and lived together for a few years as we tried to patch up our confusing lives. Perhaps with neither of us noticing, Murph took the primary role in gently leading us to a path of spiritual awakening.

We were somehow brought to the teachings of *A Course in Miracles* and shared these books in Murph's basement apartment. I lived upstairs with my mother, Phyllie, and my younger son, Kevin. Although I had claimed to be an agnostic during early adulthood, *A Course in Miracles* unexpectedly captured my heart. I became entranced by its process of spiritual mind training.

It was Murph, however, who took the lead in the study of the way of the mystics. He voraciously read both modern and ancient spiritual literature. He developed his own understanding of how to connect to his Higher Power, to the Holy Spirit, to the Source of all Creation. *A Course in Miracles* provided the leading philosophy, but he connected all the spiritual teachings to the one universal truth: **God is**. Murph became my role model for how I wanted to connect to the Voice of God.

Murph became a highly respected financial leader for Citigroup in the field of electronic options trading. I still have no idea what he actually did, but it certainly kept him very busy. He was far too busy, I thought, to write and publish a spiritual book intended to inspire and motivate a younger generation to a path of connection to Divine wisdom. He wanted more time with his family—not more work to do.

But as he explained to me, he believed his best choice was to write. His Higher Power promised He would direct the process, asking Murph for his willingness to carry out this project, with the instructions, "Write this book and I will take care of it." Murph asked, "Take care of what?" And Spirit replied, "All of it."

So Murph went to work. He wrote on the Long Island Railroad on the way to and from his high-pressure job in Manhattan. He wrote in the early mornings and late at night. He wrote somewhat effortlessly during short breaks from the responsibilities of his chaotic job. Murph was guided by Spirit and he chose to comply.

Despite occasional doubts about his ability to do this, Spirit continued to motivate him to complete the assignment. Murph developed a deep trust in following his guide. His inner voice promised, during the quiet of meditation, that he was doing valuable work.

In *The Three Rooms,* Murph is presenting ancient truths in a different form. He is helping others with a modern-day spiritual document designed to reach the younger generations to which his two sons and daughter belong.

I can't wait to see all the good that comes from this.

Larry Glenz
Ordained Ministerial Counselor
Pathways of Light
June 2016

INTRODUCTION

WE ARE ALL SLEEPWALKING. MOST OF US JUST DON'T KNOW IT yet. We are caught up in our thoughts, but we seldom monitor what we are thinking. When our thoughts are in control, we think we are in the real world. But when we awaken to our Higher Power, we become aware that we have been living in a dream world. That's why the primary purpose of every spiritual path is to awaken—awaken from the illusion of the world we see.

In his book *A New Earth*, modern-day mystic Eckhart Tolle tells us that awakening is "a shift in consciousness in which thinking and awareness separate" and that awareness is simply "our conscious connection with universal intelligence."[1] This Divine consciousness is accessible to you, me, everyone. The only thing preventing us from experiencing it is our own thoughts, which get in the way because of our lack of awareness of those very thoughts.

Tolle isn't the only one to implore us to awaken. Mystics have been telling us that for generations. Wayne Teasdale, in his descriptive book *The Mystic Heart*, points out that "each great religion has a similar origin: the spiritual awakening of its founders to God, the Divine, the absolute, the spirit, *Tao*, boundless awareness."[2] It doesn't matter if we're talking about Buddha, Muhammad, Moses, Jesus, Lao Tzu, or any other spiritual master. They all had one thing in common: they had a spiritual awakening. If we want to experience what they did, we need to ask ourselves: What did they awaken from?

To answer this question, we must learn to differentiate between our common assumptions of the real world and the dream world. If you ask any person walking down the street, "What is the real world?" they may say, "It's when you are awake, or when you are conscious." Most people believe the real world to be the physical world (otherwise known as the world of form) that is full of things that we can see. If you ask them, "What is the dream world?" they may tell you, "It's when you are sleeping, or when you are unconscious." The dream world is typically believed to be the unseen world (known as the world of light). Finally, if you ask them about sleepwalking, they will often say, "It's when you are walking around in the physical world but you are still dreaming." This is not the kind of sleepwalking I am talking about.

If we already live in the physical world, which we believe to be the real world, then awakening to this world doesn't make any sense. We are already here. The only way we can wake up *from* the physical world is if this isn't the real world, after all. Only if the world of form is really the dream state can we awaken from it into the real world, which is the world of light. That's what the mystics have been telling us all along. We need to look around at what we see in the physical world and shift our perception so that we are aware of this world of forms being the dream—because that's what the physical world is. It's our perception of reality.

When we go to bed at night, what we think and how we feel when we are falling asleep can affect what we dream about. When we "wake up," those dreams feel real to us. They feel like they really happened. The same principle applies in the physical world. What we think and how we feel in the physical world affects what we perceive is happening to us—and that perception is unique to each one of us. That is why two people can witness the same event and each come away with a completely different interpretation of that experience. What they perceived to be happening was based on what they were thinking and feeling at the time of the event, and that became their perception of reality. Even if those perceptions were different, they were real for each one of them. Therefore, what we create in the physical world and what we create in the non-physical world are based on what we perceive to be real.

Most people will resist the idea that what they are looking at in the physical world is actually the dream. They'll say, "It can't be a dream; it feels too real." Well, a dream can feel pretty real too. One night I went into my daughter's room because she was having a nightmare. After she calmed down, she said, "Dad, you know when you are in a dream, you feel like you are actually in it." Even a six-year-old can recognize that a dream feels real.

So what is our purpose here on earth? It is to awaken. It is to align with our Higher Self so we can live the lives we desire. Well, open your eyes and see through the eyes of Source. Awaken from the dream. As Henry David Thoreau put it, "Our truest life is when we are in dreams awake."[3]

What can I say on the subject that is any different from what you may have heard before? I'm just someone who's been on his own spiritual journey for the past twenty years, and I've learned there is not much anyone can say that is brand new. What I *can* do is tell you the same things in a different way.

Back in school, were you ever taught something over and over until you thought you understood it, then a new teacher showed you a different way to view the problem, and all of a sudden you had an "aha" moment? Something just clicked, and the problem made total sense? Because the truth is the truth, it has been passed down by mystics from generation to generation. I have no new secrets to reveal that will transform your life, just some old secrets to present to you in a different way. Why is this valuable? Because we all have different triggers for remembering concepts, and that's what this process is really all about—remembering. It's about going back to where we came from. It's about connecting with our Source.

Sometimes we use things like stickers or sticky notes to remind us of what we need to do. Hopefully, you'll find some "stickers" in this book to remind you of how to get home. But don't get hung up on every sticker. As they say in Al-Anon, "Take what you like and leave the rest."[4] My deepest wish is that *The Three Rooms* can help many different groups of people over time, such as those suffering from addiction and depression, and those who are just plain unhappy with their lives.

When writing this book, I tried to relay the inner voice of my Higher Self, or that universal consciousness that we all share. If

I've been successful, you will not hear the voice of my Higher Self but of *your* Higher Self because those voices are the same voice. If you find fault in what I am saying, then ask yourself where the doubt is coming from. As long as this doubt comes from your inner conscience, and not from what others have told you to be true, it is okay. There is no right or wrong, just what is true for each of us, and that truth comes from within. Ideally, you will find that you experience these words as if they are coming from your Higher Self, and they can be as true for you as they are for me.

It is important to note that you, the reader, need not believe in God or a Divine presence in order to benefit from the concepts of *The Three Rooms*. By simply separating your awareness from your thoughts, you can begin to awaken, or at least improve your experience of life. For me, a belief in a Higher Power just makes it a lot easier.

Ultimately, we are all sleepwalking because we focus on what we think, what we hear, and what we see. Because we are conscious of those sensations, they seem real to us. But if we recognize those thoughts, words, and objects as things outside of us, then we no longer identify with them—and they cannot control how we feel. Once these things no longer control us, we remember who we are. We are not the thoughts, the words, or the objects that we get so consumed with. We are the ones watching the thoughts, the words, and the objects. When we allow them to consume us, then we have slipped back into the dream. When we become aware of them, then we have woken up.

CHAPTER 1

WHERE ARE YOU?

PEOPLE ON A SPIRITUAL PATH FREQUENTLY ASK THEMSELVES, "Who am I?" It is an iconic question that has been asked for generations. The answers can only be revealed when we look within—but that's not where we usually look.

We generally define who we are in the physical world by what other people see—our appearance, our occupation, or our possessions. But who we are on the outside always changes. I am a steelworker. Now I am unemployed. I'm dating a waitress. Now she dumped me for another man. We call this life. The Eastern cultures call it *maya*, which is just another name for all the crap that goes on in our external lives.

If all our attention is focused on the image we want others to see, we will never discover the person on the inside that only we can see. Who we are on the inside never changes. It is our eternal being, the part of us that others can't see. So when you ask yourself, "Who am I?" you need to clarify whether you mean the "I" that everyone else sees or the "I" that only you see.

You also need to differentiate between the internal and external self when you answer the question, "Where am I?" In the physical world, whenever we don't pay attention to where we're going, we get lost. Once we realize we're lost, we focus and eventually find our way back to our destination. Depending on how long we were distracted, we could be a few blocks off course or we could be miles away. Fortunately, this doesn't happen often, because there are landmarks to help us monitor where we're going. That is not the case with the non-physical world.

Our thoughts can come and go as quickly as objects do when we drive down a highway at fifty miles per hour. Furthermore, we pay far more attention to the objects we see than to our thoughts. We are accustomed to monitoring what we see, but not what we think. As a result, we get lost in our thoughts far more often than we get lost in the physical world, and since we rarely pay attention to the direction of our thoughts, we can get lost for long periods of time without realizing it.

It is helpful to monitor your thoughts, because where your attention is directed determines how you will answer the question, "Who am I?" If you focus on the external world, you will identify with the person everyone else sees. If you look internally, you will identify with the person only you can see. That is your eternal being. It's your true self. You will never discover who you truly are if your thoughts are concentrated on external objects. In order to answer the question, "*Who* am I?" you must first answer an even more fundamental question: "*Where* am I?"

We need to ask ourselves, "Where am I?" all day, every day. The more we commit to asking this simple question, the more time we will spend knowing who we really are instead of battling with the ego. When you silently ask yourself, "Where am I?" you are really asking, "Where are my thoughts?"

Anybody walking down the street can tell you where your physical body is. You can ask a stranger, "Hey, you, where am I?" You may get a response—"You're at Thirty-third and Second." Great, now you know where your body is. But your thoughts are someplace else. You're at Thirty-third Street and Second Avenue in New York City, yet in your mind you're still wallowing in misery over something that happened two days ago. Anyone can tell you where you are on the outside. Only you can answer where you are on the inside.

Use the same diligence to monitor your thoughts as you do to monitor your physical whereabouts. The more you ask yourself, "Where am I?" the closer you'll get to discovering who you are.

Where Can You Be?

We know we can physically be in only one place at a time. However, mentally traveling to the past or future is not only possible but something we do constantly, at warp speed, without even knowing it. A friend may tell you about their trip around the country and BAM! You start thinking about the argument you had with your wife last week about vacation plans. Then they bring up a college they visited with their daughter and WHAM! You worry about how you are going to pay for your son's future college education. With our thoughts, time travel is not only possible but seemingly inevitable. Unlike the physical body, our thoughts can be in one of three places, and each place leads to a different experience of life.

THE PAST ROOM

One of the most common places our thoughts go is the past. We think of events that have already happened and relive the feelings we experienced at that time and place. Past experiences can remind us of what we perceive other people to have done to us, and often these thoughts produce unpleasant emotions. To make matters worse, rather than recognizing that they make us feel bad, we tend to dwell on those thoughts, which further perpetuates the negative emotions they generate. "Learning" from the past may be a necessary endeavor, but continuing to relive emotions that make us feel bad is not useful.

THE FUTURE ROOM

Our physical bodies may not be able to jump ahead in time, but we have no problem thinking way ahead about what might happen in the future. We create different scenarios for how our experience in the physical world may unfold. Usually, we come up with worst-case scenarios, which are not pretty. This is not the same as planning for the future, in which we envision positive outcomes in our lives. Instead, our thoughts often run ahead into the future and focus on all the things that could go wrong in the world. These thoughts do not make us feel good.

So our thoughts can go backward in the linear concept of

time (the Past Room) or they can go forward (the Future Room). But what if they don't go in either direction?

THE PRESENT ROOM

The only other place our thoughts can be is right here in the present. When our thoughts are in the present, we can't relive negative emotions from the past or feel anxious about how we think our life may unfold. When we are in the present moment, we experience no thoughts based on our perception of time and space, because we are focused on only one point in time: now. In this moment, and only in this moment, we are aligned with the vibrational frequency of our Source. This is Divine consciousness. In this room, we feel love.

UNDERSTANDING OUR VIBRATIONAL FREQUENCY

As science continues to evolve, we have a better understanding of the relationship between the physical and non-physical world. Everything we see and hear in the physical world is just us interpreting the vibrations of light waves and sound waves that we receive. Similarly, what we think and feel in the non-physical world is based on our interpretation of the vibrations we receive. Our Higher Self vibrates at the same frequency as Source Energy itself. That is the frequency we want to tune in to. That frequency is called love.

We can use an emotional scale to actually monitor the vibrational frequency of our emotions, or how we feel. But our feelings are influenced by our thoughts and perceptions. So what is a thought, and where does it go after we receive it?

A thought is a vibration that is stored as energy in a Field of Potential Probabilities, waiting to manifest.

This field of energy has had many names. Sometimes it is called Divine consciousness, prana, or the Akashic field. Other times it is called the quantum vacuum, ether, or the zero point field. No matter what name you apply to it, it is the Source energy that makes up *all there is*.

So, just as we are constantly interpreting vibrations we receive in the physical world, we are also constantly interpreting vibrations we receive in the non-physical world. All of the inspired ideas we receive, as well as the negative thoughts we produce, are stored in the same Field of Potential Probabilities. It is up to us to determine which ones we access based on the vibrations we are producing in any moment. That is what determines our ability to communicate with our Higher Power.

When our emotions resonate with the same vibrational frequency as our Higher Self, we are able to interpret those vibrations in the form of inspired ideas. This is what happens when our thoughts are in the Present Room.

When our emotions are not in alignment with our Higher Self, we are interpreting vibrations based on what we see and hear in the form of resistant thoughts. This is what happens when our thoughts are in the Past or Future Room.

The Act of Observation

Unfortunately, most of us are trapped in the Past or Future Room without even realizing it. We are too absorbed in day-to-day trivialities to stop and take the time to observe—observe our thoughts, our feelings, and our behavior.

Over the last century, science and religion have finally begun to join the same team. During the seventeenth century, they were fierce competitors for the title of Explainer of the Universe. They each developed a loyal following who remained steadfast in their separate beliefs until the nineteenth century, when they started to come together. It was Albert Einstein who said, "Science without religion is lame, religion without science is blind."[1] Many ancient spiritual teachings have stressed that awareness is the key to accessing our Higher Power, which is the consciousness behind everything we see and feel. Now quantum physics, due to the Copenhagen interpretation in the 1920s, is telling us the act of observation is the key to the formation of physical matter—everything we see and feel.

Observation and awareness are interchangeable. Awareness is the key to higher consciousness, and the act of observing is all about awareness. Because awareness is how we connect to the intelligence of the universe, there is no better meditation than the act of observation. It is the quickest way to join forces with Divine consciousness—and, after all, that is what meditation is all about.

The key is to be aware of yourself as an observer and not of what you are observing. If you focus on what you are observing, you will attract more of that into your life—whether you like it or not. If you focus on the observer, which is your eternal being, then you will be aware of your Source and will attract more of what you desire into your life.

OBSERVING YOUR THOUGHTS

If you are going to observe anything, looking inside your head is a good place to start. As you will read later in this book, our lives are like movies playing in a theater. They can either be dramas (Past or Future Movies) or romantic comedies (the Present Movie). When we get caught up in the drama, we become actors in the scene, without awareness of the part we play. But when we remove ourselves from that drama and observe it as the audience, then we can participate in the movie of our life with full awareness of our Higher Self.

To this end, you need to be the gatekeeper to those things that may keep you from that awareness—your thoughts. Observing your thoughts means watching them come into your mind, acknowledging them, and if they make you feel good, holding on to them. If they make you feel bad, release them. Loving thoughts will bring you closer to your awareness of Divine consciousness, while all non-loving thoughts will move you further away. For some reason, most of us have that backward. As loving thoughts come into our minds, we tend to say something like, "Oh, that's nice" and release them. But when non-loving thoughts come into our minds, we tend to say something like, "I can't believe what that S.O.B. did to me!" and proceed to hold on to those non-loving thoughts for dear life. That's not what the masters teach us to do.

While there are distinct differences between the Christian and Buddhist faiths, they also share a lot of common ground, such as their emphasis on observing our thoughts. Many good comparisons are contained in Thich Nhat Hanh's enlightening book *Living Buddha, Living Christ*.[2] In the King James Bible, Proverbs 23:7 says, "For as he thinks in his heart, so is he."[3] This is widely interpreted as "As you think, so shall you be." In essence, Christ is saying there is nothing more important than monitoring our thoughts.

As our entire being is dependent on what we think, you'd think we would pay more attention to our thoughts. In the Buddhist faith, they call this mindfulness, which is interpreted as the intentional awareness of your thoughts in the present moment. This awareness brings you into the present moment, just as the act of observation brings together physical matter. But mindfulness is a gradual process to eventually master. We need reminders throughout the day to keep observing our thoughts and creating awareness.

Becoming more aware of your thoughts in each moment doesn't mean you'll never do anything stupid again, or that you won't have thoughts about attacking someone for something you think they have done to you. But you will notice those dumb things you do, and you will notice those non-loving thoughts, and you will begin to smile at how ridiculous they are.

OBSERVING YOUR BEHAVIOR

How would you describe yourself? Think of all the characteristics you believe you possess. Now, how would others describe you? Would they list the same characteristics?

We often see ourselves completely differently from how

others view us. That is why it is imperative that we observe our own behavior—constantly. Opportunities to do this crop up all day. Perhaps you're driving your car and someone cuts you off. You may honk your horn and yell, "Watch it, you jerk!" The next day, when you unintentionally cut someone else off and they honk their horn and yell at you, your response might be, "What's your problem?" We do stuff like this all the time. We notice what other people do to us but rarely notice that we do the same to others. The only way we will notice is to start to observe our own behavior.

All the great mystics have taught us about spiritual truths and implored us to remember them—not to remember the human being who told us about these truths, like Lao Tzu, Jesus, or Siddhartha, but to remember their teachings that expressed who they really were inside. We want to focus on their behavior because they lived their lives in accordance with their teachings; that is to say, they lived their truths. When you remember them, you understand their behavior reflected their teachings. The question to ask yourself is, "How will *I* be remembered?" To answer that question, you need to learn to observe your own behavior, to see how others perceive you. Once you start the process, you become the witness to everything you say and do. Now you begin to get a glimpse of how you will be remembered.

OBSERVATION VS. JUDGMENT

As we develop the habit of observing our thoughts and behaviors, we inevitably start to observe the behavior of others. But observing other people's actions in the world of form invariably leads us to interpret what we see within the context of our own experience. Herein lies one of the most challenging aspects of any spiritual path: learning to observe without judgment.

Observing what others do without judging them takes a lot more than practice. It takes an understanding of why we judge people in the first place. When people say, "I don't judge others," they mean they don't *consciously* judge. Your ego doesn't want you to know you are judging others, but we all do it in subtle ways. We make assumptions all the time. If we see someone driving a car, we immediately assume they own it. Consequently, we make judgments about that person depending solely on which type of car they are driving.

We judge people when they have too much and we judge them when they have too little. We can't help ourselves. We think we know them based on what we see on the outside. We make assumptions about them based on where they live or what they do for a living. But houses and careers don't define people. Outward trappings aren't what sustain them on the inside, and we don't know them on the inside. All we know is what we see on the outside—what they're wearing or the color of their skin—and we think that tells us everything about that person. This is stereotyping. We have just placed them into a preconceived category, but in reality, the bucket that we just placed that person in exists only in our own mind. It is a false image of who they are.

If we are going to stereotype someone, which is just creating an oversimplified image of them, then we should picture them as an eternal being who has manifested in their physical body—which is what we all are. Then their outward appearance doesn't change our perception of who they are on the inside. When we recognize others as our own self externalized, then all judgments are dissolved. We feel more confident putting someone in a bucket when we actually observe their behavior, but even that can lead to a false judgment. For instance, suppose you see two people in a heated debate and one of them is clearly acting more aggressive. Although you can't hear the conversation, you immediately come to the conclusion that one of them is acting like a real jerk. You are quite certain that person is obnoxious and demanding. Why are you so sure? Because you saw their behavior with your own eyes. But any magician knows that what people see is not always what is really happening. What people see is just an illusion. There is always something else going on behind the scenes. So don't get caught up in the illusion of other people's behavior when you don't know the reason for it.

Imagine if the person you thought was obnoxious and demanding was really a distraught mother arguing with a hospital admissions director to get her sick child treatment for a life-threatening illness because she refuses to accept there is no help for her daughter. Would she still be a jerk? Of course not. You made a judgment based on what you saw with your own eyes, but you didn't know the whole picture. People can't know the whole picture with other people, not just in that situation but in millions of others. So next time you start to make a judgment based on what you see, ask yourself how you can possibly know the whole story. You can't. So, see beyond someone's behavior. Try to see beyond their exterior to who they really are on the inside, even if they've forgotten who they really are.

OPINIONS ARE NOT THE TRUTH

Sometimes we make judgments and our ego convinces us that these are "just my opinions." But opinions are the cousins of judgments, and like judgments, opinions are not the truth. Opinions and judgments in and of themselves are not bad. We need to make judgments every day about safety and other issues. But judgments and opinions that damage other people are quite different. Very often they are based on incomplete or inaccurate information. But still, we let the opinions of others bother us so much. We wonder what people think about us and what they will say about us. But there are over seven billion people on this planet. If you're hoping for all seven billion to have a positive opinion about you, you're setting yourself up for constant disappointment.

We make assumptions and form opinions when we observe other people, and these are both types of judgment. But the act of observation itself is absent of judgment. If our focus is on the observer, then we just observe. To form a judgment, we need to interpret what we see. That interpretation is based on our individual perceptions. The problem is that we often base our perceptions on faulty information, on what we *think we see* and not on what we *know*.

In reality, there are only two things we see, and they are not seen with the physical eye: We either see other people as aligned with the same Source energy as ourselves, or we see them as separate people. Only when we see them as they truly are—as ourselves—does all judgment melt away.

KNOWLEDGE VS. PERCEPTION

We think we know what is going on around us, but this is often just our *perception* of what is going on, which can be so strong that we believe it to be true. But if that perception is wrong, then everything else based on it is also wrong. *A Course in Miracles* is a self-study program of spiritual psychotherapy, the purpose of which is the attainment of happiness and peace through the experience of forgiveness. The course defines a miracle as a shift in perception from fear to love; only the love is real. The course also makes a clear distinction between knowledge and perception. We confuse these concepts all the time.

How can our perception be wrong? First, when our thoughts are in the Past or Future Rooms, our perception is rooted in time and space and based on our projection of who we think we are in that time and space. We see others as separate people and can't help but focus on our perceived differences. Knowledge, on the other hand, comes from being aligned with our Higher Self in the Present Room, and it doesn't buy into that illusion. It does not recognize a world of duality, of time and space. It only recognizes the truth, which is our oneness with the Source of all living things. Therefore, our (mis)perceptions of ourselves and others are not based on knowledge. They are an illusion we experience until we "remember" the truth. That is why *A Course in Miracles* so eloquently states, "Knowledge preceded both perception and time, and will ultimately replace them. That is the real meaning of 'Alpha and Omega,' the beginning and the end."[4]

In addition to time and space, we base our perceptions on a belief in separation. Many of us believe we are separate individuals with no common connection to our Source. In reality, if one of us is connected to our Source, then we are all connected to it, whether we realize it or not. That is the Divine consciousness that we all share. Everything else is illusion. This is not to say that there is no such thing as a physical world with other human beings in it because, clearly, we can look around and see other people. The key is that, inside, we are no different from everyone else.

The belief in separation and duality is based on what we see with our eyes. The concept of oneness, or Divine consciousness, is based on what we feel with our hearts. We see our differences in the physical world, but we feel our oneness in the non-physical world. Therefore, as long as we continue to focus on the physical world, we will remain convinced we are all separate beings. Only when we feel our connection to our Source will we recognize we all share that same feeling: love. And as the Dalai Lama says, "Love is the absence of judgment."[5]

The belief that you are separate from anyone else is a false assumption, and it is only experienced in the Past or Future Rooms. The negative emotions that you feel about someone are your indicator that you are not perceiving that person the same way your Higher Self perceives them, and consequently, you are in the wrong room. If you stop believing in the concept of separation, you will stop believing in the concept of judgment, and if you don't believe in judging, you can't be judged. That is what Christ meant when he said, "Judge not, lest ye be judged."[6] He didn't mean people will stop judging you if you don't judge them but that you will stop *feeling* judged. Likewise, the more you judge others, the more you will feel judged by them. The irony is that people who judge others will feel judged even when they are not being judged by others, and people who don't judge won't feel judged by others, even when they are being judged.

WHERE'S GOD?

An extension of judgment is blame. We tend to believe there is nothing wrong with us. Anything not going right in our lives is almost always someone else's fault. "Did you see what he did to me?" "Did you hear what she said?" "What was she thinking?" On a grander scale, we always have God to blame. With so much human suffering in the world, we think surely God has abandoned us.

In 1987, Martin Handford wrote *Where's Waldo?*, which captured the imagination of millions of children and their parents.[7] The concept was simple. In very detailed pictures of public settings, such as crowded malls or train stations, the author hid a young man named Waldo. When you glance at the scene, Waldo blends in and is difficult to locate. But you know, indisputably, that he's there, right in front of your eyes, even if you can't spot him. The same can be said for God. He is always right there, in every scene of your life; you just can't always recognize him. He blends in. The fact that you haven't found him doesn't mean he's not there. You're just not looking in the right place.

The search for God is even more challenging when you watch the nightly news and nine out of ten stories are tragedies of some kind. I remember years ago as a child, I would watch scenes of the Vietnam War on television in our living room as we waited for dinner. Every generation has to endure its own hardships and tragedies, and dig deep down inside as the outside world gets a little too difficult to bear. This seems especially true today. We also experience challenges on a smaller scale, when things don't seem to go our way. Often little things go wrong during the course of the day and we want to blame someone, even God. In truth, blaming other people is the same as blaming God.

Most of the time, we wait to blame the big things on God or use them as evidence that he doesn't exist. When we're dealing with famine, wars, and tragedies of all kinds, we ask each other, "Where's God during all of this?" Or else we think, "How could God let these things happen?" The reality is that God doesn't allow bad things to happen; we do. He also never abandons us; we just can't always find him. The quickest way to find our creator is to look within. But that doesn't mean we can't find evidence of God out in the physical world, as well. Like Waldo, he has blended into the daily scenes of our lives.

So what are we looking for? Most of us no longer expect to find a guy with a long white beard and flowing robe. It has been said that God is love, so let's start there. Every time you witness a demonstration of love, you have just found God. If you have trouble finding such a demonstration, then simply give one yourself. Every act of kindness that you or anyone else performs is a demonstration of love. It is your proof that God is always with us. Finding love in yourself or others is the same as finding God.

SEARCH FOR MEANING AND SEE WHAT YOU FIND

Such a search is not just about finding evidence of God all around us. We need to find meaning in our own lives. If you find that difficult because of challenges you're currently facing in your life, read about others who had to deal with tremendous hardships and refused to play the part of the victim. Dr. Viktor Frankl, an Austrian psychiatrist, is one of those inspirational people. In his book *Man's Search for Meaning*, he describes how he and his family were wrenched from their home in 1942 and sent to concentration camps.[8] His family were all killed, and he suffered unspeakable daily atrocities at Auschwitz. If anyone ever had reasons to be bitter and resentful about life, it was him. But Frankl didn't see it that way. Instead, he saw examples of God at work each and every day. These may have been little acts of kindness obscured by all the torture and suffering, but they were there. Only when you become aware of God's presence in every moment of your life can you begin to find your true meaning.

When you read Frankl's story, you realize that every encounter we have with another human being has the potential to be a holy one. Frankl teaches us that meaning in life can occur by experiencing other human beings in their uniqueness—and by loving them. Love is the only way to truly understand another human being at his or her core. None of us can become fully aware of the very essence of another human being unless we love them. Frankl came to see the interconnectedness of us all. When we learn to see this, we strengthen both our level of compassion and our capacity to love. Most relevant here, though, is that Frankl found God in the darkest scenes of his life, where most others would have stopped looking.

If Frankl could find meaning in his life and evidence of God in a Nazi concentration camp, then there should be no scenario in your life where you can't do the same. There is no place that you are and God is not. Reminders are everywhere; you will find them in books, poems, movies, and songs. Each one will help to provide you with your own experience of God. But you need to look with diligence. When you listen to exceptional achievers, they always talk about the effort that goes into becoming a great performer. As legendary coach Paul "Bear" Bryant said, "It's not the will to win that matters—everyone has that. It's the will to prepare to win that matters."[9] It's all about the effort you put into preparing yourself to become that which you aspire to be.

Spiritual masters are no different. They didn't just wake up one day as enlightened beings. They all exhibited a tremendous desire to get to know their Higher Self. If you have that passion, they have given you the blueprint to follow, to access the same Divine consciousness they did and move back into the Present Room.

Let's take a deeper look into each of the Three Rooms.

CHAPTER 2

THE PAST ROOM

HOW OFTEN HAVE YOU WISHED YOU COULD HAVE A "DO-OVER"? If you could just go back to yesterday, for example, and have that conversation with your son again, you may think that surely you would say the right things this time. You ask yourself, "What was I thinking when I said that?" or "What was I thinking when I did that?" Sometimes we need to retrieve certain memories, but more often than not, when we visit the Past Room, it is to dwell on things we have previously said or done. But these visits don't physically transport us back in time, and good things don't usually result from dwelling on past actions.

How many times have you heard someone say about someone else, "Stay away from him, he's in a really bad place" or "Watch out for her, she's not herself today"? You might agree, because you can see the person seething with negative emotions and apparently acting irrationally, not like "themselves." But what does it mean when we say someone is in a "bad place"? Not that they drove to the corner drug store in a bad part of town, but that they are absorbed in negative thoughts, perhaps stewing about things that happened in the past and unable to focus on the present. They are not aligned with their eternal being. In other words, they are stuck in the Past Room and they don't know it. And when our thoughts are lost in the Past Room, we are assailed by all kinds of not-so-fun stuff, like guilt, anger, vengeful urges, and resentment.

UNDERSTANDING RESENTMENT

Let's start with resentment. It is an all-consuming, uncomfortable emotion. Like all emotions, resentment can result from conscious or subconscious thoughts or beliefs. But this emotion can only surface when you focus on things outside of you. It may be something a neighbor has that you wish you possessed, or a comment a coworker made that hurt your feelings, or even just that your friend appears to be two clothing sizes smaller than you. Whatever the specific trigger, resentment can consume you. Once consumed by this emotion, your thoughts become fixated on it and you can't get out of the Past Room.

That's the problem with visiting the Past Room. You think you're having a few harmless thoughts, but they start to generate powerful negative emotions, which cause you to dwell on the thoughts that got you there, and around and around you go. This is not an enjoyable merry-go-round. Why do you usually feel unpleasant emotions in the Past Room? Because it is where you store the negative energies you have prevented from flowing naturally through your body. This energy includes all the things people did that you didn't appreciate and all the things they said that rubbed you the wrong way. These are all the things that don't match your concept of who you are.

You have formed your own beliefs about how people should behave, and when they don't behave that way, you hang on to their offenses and store them in the Past Room. When people make declarations like, "I'll forgive but I won't forget" or "He's never going to do that to me again," it's clear they've saved these slights in order to revisit them in the Past Room. When you store such memories instead of letting them go, any time an event occurs that bears the slightest resemblance to that perceived injustice done to you (perhaps years ago), it immediately leads you back to the Past Room, where you're guaranteed to resurrect all the negative emotions you felt the first time around. And so the cycle continues: new event—Past Room (which is the same as action—reaction). Instead of watching each new event come into your life with an open mind, you jump back into the Past Room so you can taste that bitterness again and again.

This is not to be confused with recalling positive past experiences. Those pleasant memories will always bring you back to the Present Room. Thoughts about the past that make you feel good are due to you perceiving that experience the same way your Higher Self has always perceived it. Since your Higher Self is always in the Present Room, recalling positive past experiences will always bring you back there. The Past Room, on the other hand, is when you are perceiving something from your past that is not in alignment with how your Higher Self has perceived the same event. The Past Room is simply a collection of all the things you've done that have not made you feel good and all the perceived negative things others have done to you. In other words, the Past Room is the sum total of the negative thoughts you refuse to let go about yourself.

THE GUILT TRIP

The United States has a judicial system as good as any in the world. There is a set of societal laws designed to keep the citizens safe. If someone is accused of breaking the law, they are entitled to a jury of their peers to determine their innocence. But if it is decided that they broke one of these laws, they are judged guilty and face the consequences. They are sentenced to a punishment depending on the severity of the crime, ranging from something as light as a monetary fine up to something as heavy as years in prison. Criminals, or those who have committed crimes against other members of society, go through a process of being judged by their peers as either innocent or guilty, and little compassion is typically exhibited to those found guilty.

We also live by a moral code we must adhere to, which is not the same as the societal laws. This moral code is a set of personal guidelines. Spiritual teachings often act as a moral guide for us as well. The Ten Commandments are a moral code many people live by. Some of these moral codes overlap with societal laws, such as "Thou shalt not kill," but other moral codes can be broken without breaking societal laws, such as lying, cheating, and coveting thy neighbor's wife. You can think all you want about your neighbor's wife, but you won't be found guilty of a crime in a court of law even if such thoughts make you feel guilty inside. Once you have internalized moral integrity, you don't need societal laws to tell you what is right or wrong.

However, even though everyone has different ideas of right and wrong, and we all know when we break our own code, others may accuse us of breaking *their* moral code, which might not match yours. This is how people can make you feel guilty even if you don't think you've done anything wrong.

CONTRASTING CODES LEAD TO GUILT

Say you're excited about an upcoming trip and you tell a friend, "I can't wait; Bob and I are getting away from our children and taking a quick trip to the country this weekend." What if instead of getting a response like, "Hey, that's great" or "Have fun," your friend says, "Why would you do that?" or "What about the kids? Is that fair to them?" Goodbye good feeling, hello guilt. Your friend has no idea what is going on in your life; they are projecting their concept of who they think you should be on to you. You have a choice, though. You can accept how that friend thinks you should behave and therefore feel guilty about your actions, or you can follow your own conscience.

SELF-CREATED GUILT

Let's assume you are following your own conscience and not that of others. That's great—until it isn't. We may think someone is mad at us based on something we said, and we feel guilty about having said it, even though they were never angry with us. When it comes to guilt, we are masters at creating it by ourselves. Not only that, but we can be far more vicious to ourselves than someone else might be. Sometimes we feel guilty based on what someone else says or does, even when it was not their intention. We look into the Past Room, relive all the things we think we should have done differently, and dump loads of guilt on ourselves.

GUILT BREEDS MISERY

We have all heard the expression "Misery loves company." The root of all misery is guilt, and guilt loves company too! So we project our subconscious guilt on to others to make ourselves feel better. This may work momentarily, but it only succeeds in making us feel guiltier because we haven't been completely freed of the guilt. Thus, around and around we go. The fascinating part is that we usually don't realize we are doing this because we don't see that we are projecting guilt on to ourselves. We beat ourselves up without being aware of it, and then we feel justified in making others feel guilty because it feels so natural.

We have all heard the saying "Dogs are a man's best friend." Why is that? Maybe it's because they don't project their subconscious guilt on to us. That's because dogs can't feel guilt. They can only feel sad if we yell at them or forget to take them for a walk. As a result, we feel great love and compassion from them. If we would like other people to feel love and compassion from us, maybe we should take our cue from dogs and eliminate guilt from our lives.

SEPARATION BREEDS GUILT

The reason other people can make us feel guilty is that we believe we are separate from them. We forget that we are all connected to the same Source. But real guilt comes when we forget our own connection to our Source. This guilt grows subconsciously, because our minds may not be processing the fact that our egos have disconnected from our Higher Self and we feel guilty about it. But deep down inside, there is an awareness that something big is lacking in our lives. We just can't put our finger on what it is. When we start to understand that separation from God's love is an illusion, all guilt is dissolved, both conscious and subconscious.

THE BLAME GAME

It's so easy to blame someone else when something goes wrong in our lives. We shout, "It's his fault!" Humans do this every day in our personal lives, at all levels of business and government, and between nations. Sometimes the blame game goes on so long that the blamer loses track of what the person they're blaming did in the first place. This is why long-simmering feuds never get resolved.

LEARNING TO BLAME OTHERS

On a personal level, the blame game often starts in childhood. Although we are born in pure innocence, at an early age we learn when it is beneficial to say, "I did it" and when it is more advantageous to say, "She did it." For example, when a parent comes in the playroom and says, "Oh, wonderful, who put the toys away?" children quickly learn that when they answer, "I did it," they'll get a reward, even if it's only their mother's beaming face. Positive behavior rarely gets blamed on someone else. Conversely, if a parent walks into the room and sees a broken lamp on the rug and angrily exclaims, "Who broke this?" most children will be sorely tempted to point to their younger brother and say, "He did it." If the child is telling the truth, that's fine. But when children knowingly place the blame on someone else to avoid unpleasant consequences, they are going against their intuitive, innocent nature. This is a learned behavior, and one we don't always unlearn later in life. Why do we cross this line? At what point do we turn from innocent to deceitful?

BLAMING OTHERS WITH OUR THOUGHTS

Very often we fail to take responsibility for not only our actions but also our thoughts. So it's important to become aware of when we project our negative associations on to others. For example, you may be talking to a friend when another acquaintance walks up. You say, "Hi," but your friend gives him an uninviting scowl. The acquaintance obviously feels the animosity toward him and walks away. You look at your friend, and he says, "What? I didn't say anything." But he could have some unresolved issues with the acquaintance that led to his nonverbal grimace. He doesn't realize mental projections are just as powerful as words. As author John C. Maxwell says, "People may hear your words, but they feel your attitude."[1] Moreover, our mental projections are often based on faulty assumptions rather than on direct personal experience. These assumptions may stem from something we read or heard from someone else. So, in the example above, your friend may never have met your acquaintance but might have made an assumption about him based on hearsay.

We make these assumptions all the time. It's especially convenient when we don't want to take responsibility for something that we said or did. We instead blame it on someone else based on false assumptions, perhaps even assumptions we have made up to harm someone else and get us off the hook. It is always much easier to blame someone you don't know than someone you do, just as it's easier to blame someone who is not there to defend themselves. Ultimately, we need to realize there is only one person to blame for where we are in life: ourselves. People may do cruel things to us in this life, and tragedy can befall us, but only we control our thoughts and attitudes about what happens to us.

Why do we have so much trouble getting out of the Past Room? In our minds, what happened in the past is usually someone else's fault, and we're stuck there because of what we believe they did to us.

This doesn't necessarily mean we come right out and accuse others. The blame shifting can be subtle. You may have put off a project at work until the last minute and now can't complete it because a coworker who has vital information for the project is not available. In this scenario, someone else ends up being the primary reason the project won't get done. You may not come right out and say, "I screwed up because of him," but you might imply it despite the fact that you procrastinated. Whether explicit or implicit, the statement is the same—*It wasn't my fault!*

WE ARE NOT VICTIMS

Typically, we blame others for our own inability to take responsibility for our actions. We become the victim, and there's usually a lot of sympathy for the victim. Sometimes playing the "victim card" makes people feel better because they like the sympathy. But too often, they play the role of the victim even though they know there was nothing intentionally done to harm them. Jesus, on the other hand, was a victim of torture and murder. He could have hung on the cross and said, "You bastards are all going to rot in Hell." Instead, he said, "Father, forgive them, for they know not what they do."[2] He said that because if someone does something unloving, then they are not in their right mind, and if they are not in their right mind, how can we blame them and play the victim?

We alone can release ourselves from the past. We alone have the power to move out of the Past Room. Only when we are ready to take responsibility for our actions will we stop blaming others. When we are finally free of the blame game, we not only stop blaming others for our pain and insecurities, but we also stop feeling the need to defend ourselves.

Within *A Course in Miracles,* there is the saying "In my defenselessness my safety lies."[3] When we no longer feel the need to defend ourselves, we will no longer feel the need to blame others for anything we go through, and we can finally start to take responsibility for our own lives. We can now leave the Past Room.

ANGER MANAGEMENT

It's not hard to find humor in watching someone throw a temper tantrum. When we watch someone else lose their cool, we can see that their reaction is rarely justified by what actually happened to them. Sometimes people blow up at the littlest things and you get a good laugh—except when the person who is upset is you. Then it's not so funny. You can't step back and see the big picture, because you are too fixated on what's happening to you. The longer you're unaware that you're acting like a raving lunatic, and the more you think about the event that set you off, the longer the anger will stay with you. In other words, the longer your thoughts stay in the Past Room, the longer you will be subject to its potential consequences. Anger is one of them.

Sometimes when you are overreacting, you are aware that you're behaving in an irrational manner but you can't stop yourself from doing so. While you can't completely stop yourself, you are recognizing your anger, and when you are aware of it, you can recover much more quickly. You are on the path to managing your anger.

Anger management means realizing we are unhappy with something that was said or done in the past because we are interpreting that experience differently than our inner being. The same can be said for when we are angry at something in the present. It is just our emotions letting us know that we are not perceiving the situation the same as our Higher Self is perceiving it. Our negative emotions, including anger, act as our guide for letting us know whether we are aligned with our Higher Self or not.

Anger isn't always triggered by other people, either. We can also be mad with ourselves because of something we said or did. But instead of dwelling on what happened, we can move our thoughts back into the Present Room, acknowledge what triggered the anger, and then find humor in the situation—or at least find humor in how we reacted. If we can find humor in other people getting angry, then we should be able to laugh at ourselves as well.

FINDING GRACE

Many times, we focus our anger on little things, like too many dishes in the kitchen sink. Fortunately, self-help author Richard Carlson taught us, "Don't sweat the small stuff." But what if it's not such small stuff? Some people have had to endure great hardships and would be within their rights to be angry and bitter, but they managed to free themselves from negative feelings. In South Africa, Nelson Mandela was held captive in a jail cell for twenty-seven years after being deemed a threat to the white man. When he finally got out, he expressed no bitterness toward the whites who had oppressed him. After his release, had his thoughts stayed in the Past Room, the resulting negative emotions would likely have prevented him from becoming the country's first black president in 1994.

It takes a great deal of self-awareness to process all the negative experiences we go through and put them in the right perspective. Sometimes we hold on to anger and resentment for a long time without realizing it. These feelings fester deep inside us and boil to the surface every time our thoughts drift back to the Past Room, affecting our behavior. Some people can't seem to overcome that deep-rooted anger and therefore never experience a true sense of peace. Others may undergo a specific experience that allows them to recognize and overcome the hidden anger they have been holding on to. Which is it for you?

RELEASE THE PAST, RELEASE THE HATE

If you don't find a way to move out of the Past Room and leave your anger behind, you run the risk of that anger turning into hate. Then you have bigger challenges. Hate is such a powerful emotion. If we came from love and will ultimately return to love, how does hatred manage to consume so many people? Whole nations learn to hate other nations. Wars are fought across the globe because of hatred passed on from generation to generation. The result is that people today may have no personal experience to make them hate another nation, yet they allow the hatred to consume them because that is what they are taught.

We see it on a personal level, too. I was walking out of the New York City subway one day and heard a woman on her phone saying, "Yeah, well, we never talk anymore. I hate her and she hates me."

How do people get to that point? If they don't talk "anymore," that means they used to be friends, or at least had a relationship where they shared things. Since then, one or both of them angered the other. Things escalated, and now their relationship could have devolved from friendship to hatred. Sadly, the loss of a good friend is not uncommon. Whatever happened, they might have not forgiven and let go and therefore relive the negative experience every time they think of each other. Even worse, when those negative thoughts resurface, they continue to produce feelings of hate.

Hate is a fear-based emotion that emanates from the Past Room when we fixate on what we perceive someone has done maliciously to us. The single biggest reason that we stay in the Past Room is that we don't know that our thoughts are fixated on previous events or beliefs we've been taught in the past. If we can't let go of those thoughts, we stay in the Past Room. We could move into the Present Room if we were able to view someone we hate with love instead of anger, which is viewing them through the eyes of the Creator. Unfortunately, most people fail to accomplish that.

FIND YOUR RECKONING

Many people are unable to let go of anger and let go of hate until they have an emotional experience, or day of reckoning, that takes them back into the Present Room. The movie *Forrest Gump* illustrates this idea well.[5] Forrest, played by Tom Hanks, has a wonderful experience of life because he doesn't try to force events but rather allows them to happen. He always seems to be in the right place at the right time. That's not the case for Lieutenant Dan, his commanding officer in the army, played by Gary Sinise. He has a preconceived idea of what his destiny should be, and when it doesn't turn out that way, he has a great deal of trouble accepting his situation. After losing both his legs in the Vietnam War and failing to become a war hero like the other men in his family, he grows angry and bitter.

Then one day, a devastating storm hits the gulf coast where they have a fishing boat. Lieutenant Dan, with no legs, perches on top of the boat's mast in the wild wind and rain, cursing God for his fate in life. Following that day of reckoning, his life turns around. He is finally able to pull his thoughts out of the Past Room, with all its anger, resentment, and bitterness. This is largely because of his association with Forrest but also because of that confrontation with the Lord.

A day of reckoning is crucial in traveling many spiritual paths because we need to let go of pent-up emotions that we don't even realize we've been holding on to. We can let go of the anger by letting go of preconceived notions about ourselves and opening up to a higher consciousness. Sometimes we need to face that higher consciousness head on.

These moments of release, like Lieutenant Dan's moment, come about when someone starts to ask deeper questions like, "Why am I suffering so much?" and "What is the cause of my suffering?" This is true even if the person is screaming in anger or frustration in their suffering, but their intention is to understand the true meaning of why the suffering is taking place. When you get to that point of frustration, you need answers from the only Source that truly knows, which is your Higher Power, or Source energy itself. Ultimately, you need to be uncomfortable enough with your life situation to seek the clarity you need to find true inner peace. This will allow you to begin the process of moving out of the Past Room.

I, too, had my day of reckoning, my own Lieutenant Dan moment. I was thirty-three years old and found myself living in a small basement apartment, going through a divorce and living without my kids. This situation was not what I had envisioned for my life, and I was mad. One night, I stood up on my bed and cursed at God at the top of my lungs. I cursed him for not letting me see my kids every night. I cursed him for taking away what I had known as my life. I cursed him for not allowing me to live the life I'd envisioned for myself. We had it out, and it was not pretty. I remember screaming, "Is that the best you got? Come on, give me more! See if I give a shit! I can take it! Let's see what you got!" By the end of my tirade, I was exhausted and collapsed on the bed. I can't say that I felt a tremendous amount of peace in that moment, but I fell into a very deep sleep. The peace would come later.

WHEN ANGER TURNS TO REVENGE

When we believe someone has done something to us or a loved one, sometimes we try to inflict the same mental or emotional pain we have felt on them. What we don't realize is that the pain we feel is self-inflicted, that perhaps someone actually did not intentionally harm us; we just perceive it that way. Perception can be as powerful as reality. It is possible that no one has harmed us, but when we assign blame to someone, we can focus on that person and how we will exact revenge.

Unfortunately, revenge rarely gets rid of the pain; it only masks it. The animated children's movie *Big Hero 6* is a perfect example of how revenge can completely change the emotions and behavior of a person whose thoughts are stuck in the Past Room.[6] In this movie, the main character, Hiro, is devastated and angered by the death of his beloved brother and is driven to do things against his true nature in order to exact revenge for his brother's death. Eventually, he realizes seeking revenge doesn't make him feel any better inside. He releases his negative emotions, embraces forgiveness, and moves to the Present Room.

Only forgiveness can completely free you from the pain. When you forgive someone for what they did, or for what you perceived they did, you start to heal. But failure to forgive traps that mental and emotional pain inside of you. You may think it's gone after you've had your revenge, but it will keep coming back every time something triggers the memory of the event that caused the pain in the first place. Forgiveness allows you to let it go. It allows you to move back into the Present Room.

When you don't let go, we call it "holding a grudge." Nothing good can come from harboring such pain, yet we often cling to it like it is a part of us.

It doesn't have to be a part of us. My friend Jonathan once told me, "Holding a grudge is like letting someone live in your mind and not charging them rent." Very simply, when we focus on the bad things we believe people have done to us, we are dwelling in the Past Room. When we are in the Present Room, we focus on the good things we perceive people have done to us because of the love we feel in our heart.

Both thought processes seem real, but our subsequent behavior is quite different. When in the Past Room, we typically want revenge and think about inflicting harm on the offending person in order to get even. When we move into the Present Room, we look to forgive, which is the surest path to eradicate the negative emotions associated with revenge. Whatever we focus on will determine which behavioral path we take. So focus on the good— or, as I once heard someone say, "Spend your time getting even with the people that did you well and not the people that did you harm."

TRIGGERS

We all have "triggers" that can set off a host of emotions. Too often, they are negative emotions that are released. These can be as simple as bumping into a former colleague who criticized your work in the past or seeing someone succeed at a task you failed at, like seeing someone doing a flip off a diving board and having it remind you of when you smashed your face into the water trying to do the same thing. Sometimes when a trigger goes off, it strikes a chord deep within us because there is an element of truth to it. Perhaps we told someone a lie, and every time we see him we feel guilty about it. We may never want to admit it, but that's why seeing that person can affect us so negatively. These triggers push us into the Past Room. Of course, some triggers evoke pleasant memories, and those are welcome. But generally, we don't want triggers to take us back into the Past Room; we want triggers to get us out.

Why would you even let negative thoughts stay in your mind and bring up emotional pain every time you think of them? Because our personal triggers are the secret keys that open the memory bank and let out these negative feelings we store in the Past Room. If painful thoughts from the past are linked to negative emotions, every time something triggers those thoughts, the negative emotions return. It's like when you push a button on a vending machine and out pops a snack. Someone pushes your internal buttons and out pops a negative emotion. Sometimes you feel the emotion without realizing what brought it up, because the thought is subconscious. But if that thought is stored in the Past Room, it will generate that negative emotion every time your buttons are pushed. The greater the trigger, the more buttons you will have. But if we learn to resolve these negative feelings wholly, the buttons will no longer work. The vending machine will run out of pain.

One familiar form of trigger is specific behavior from the people we know or love. We all have experienced someone doing something again and again that touches a nerve inside us and drives us crazy. Sometimes it can be something innocuous such as leaving the toilet seat up, and other times it can be quite serious such as challenging our integrity. These repeated actions make us upset at that person, and sometimes it makes us rant and rave to others about that person's behavior. The amazing thing about these triggers is not that they can bring us right back to a bad place in our memory banks, but that the same behavior can drive us crazy over and over again; we never seem to get used to it. But why are we so surprised when someone exhibits the same behavior for the tenth time?

We don't need to let our triggers have this power over us. Ask yourself why this trigger bothers you so much. Isn't it about time we change our own reaction to that behavior, instead of getting upset with the person for repeating it? Why do you let it keep bringing your thoughts back to the Past Room?

As long as our thoughts are stuck in the Past Room, we are continuously exposed to all the negative emotions tied to that room. You need to move your thoughts back to the Present Room.

WAR OF WORDS

One of the lessons we teach children is that "Sticks and stones may break my bones, but words will never hurt me." Don't let what other people say bother you. Simple, right? But even though we learned this as children, we don't practice it as adults. We know name-calling shouldn't bother us, but it does.

The problem is that we hold on to other people's words and let them define us. One of the reasons we let words affect us is that we think the person speaking the words knows more than we do. When we want to validate our own beliefs, we ask for someone else's opinion. If they agree with us, we feel good. If they don't, we feel bad. If they tell us they are better than us, or we are no good, we feel depressed. This is because we give the words the power to affect us. In reality, words by themselves can't hurt us; we *allow* them to hurt us. We allow other people to hurt our feelings. What does that term even mean? We can't "hurt" the way we feel. We can only allow the words someone else says to trigger negative emotions. Why? Because they dredge up fears in us that we have stored in the Past Room.

We can't know what other people are going through based solely on what we see or hear about them. Nor can they know what's going on in our lives based on what they've seen or heard about us. If we remember who we are inside, nothing anyone might say can affect us. We will never attain the peace we seek if it is dependent on what others say and do. As the great American mystic Neville Goddard so eloquently put it in *The Power of Awareness*, "When it appears that people other than yourself in your world do not act toward you as you would like, it is not due to reluctance on their part, but a lack of persistence in your assumption of your life already being as you want it to be."[7] Don't let what others say about you matter more than what you know about yourself.

That's what we do. We see things and we make assumptions, and when we share those assumptions, the result can be brutally hurtful. There is a poignant scene in the movie *Good Will Hunting* where Matt Damon's character tears into Robin Williams's character simply based on one of his paintings.[8] Robin Williams's character lost half a night of sleep that night but then fell into a deep, peaceful slumber when he realized Matt Damon's words stemmed from his own insecurities. When Williams's character remembered who he was inside, the words lost their power. You can't stop people from saying hurtful things to you, but you can stop them from affecting you. Some people will try to drag you into the Past Room with hurtful comments or behavior, but you don't have to go there.

We can have fond memories of the past and remain in the Present Room, but when we dwell on painful memories, we get thrust back into the Past Room. What is a memory anyway? As Eckhart Tolle told Oprah Winfrey, "Memories are thoughts that arise. They're not realities. Only when you believe they are real do they have power over you."[9] So, observe your thoughts, and if they don't make you feel good, try to smile and let them go. Of course, the stronger the negative emotion we experience from a memory, the more challenging it is to let it go. But regardless of the severity, your thoughts don't have power over you unless you grant them power.

Still, so many of us dwell on the past because of something we regret or want to change. But you can't correct the past by thinking in the past.

Change the Present and You'll Change the Past

The Past Room is made up of a collection of all the present moments you have ever experienced in your life. So only if you change the present moment can you change *what will later* become your past. Your thoughts have no creative powers in the past, only in the present. That is why your memories are not "real." They can only take you back to the Past Room and hold you hostage to all the negative emotions you are trying to escape from. When you're finally ready to leave the Past Room and start to feel good again, simply step back into the Present Room. Then, and only then, can you start to experience those positive feelings you so desire.

CHAPTER 3

THE FUTURE ROOM

IT'S NICE TO THINK OF THINGS WE'RE GOING TO DO IN THE future. The anticipation is almost as enjoyable as the experience itself. But too often, when our thoughts get caught up in the Future Room, we start to fear all the things we imagine could go wrong. The trouble is, even when those bad things *don't* happen, we rarely look back and see how much time we wasted worrying instead of enjoying the moment.

This type of thinking is not to be confused with planning for the future. If I think it's going to rain today, I'll bring an umbrella to work. I prepare for what might happen as best as I can, then I let it go. I don't worry all day long about whether it might rain. I can't control the weather. Once I've done what I can, I let go of any further concern about it. But we're all very practiced at planning for the future and then worrying about it anyway.

Human beings are the only living creatures who imagine worst-case scenarios instead of simply allowing our lives to unfold. As a result, our ego-projected thoughts and worries create lots of negative feelings that we get to experience when we're in the Future Room. They include beauties like stress, anxiety, and depression—and they are all rooted in fear.

IMAGINATION

Having an imagination is not a bad thing, but in the Future Room, we often use it to envision all the things that could prevent us from achieving what we desire. Not surprisingly, we then attract into our lives exactly what we imagined would go wrong. In effect, we bring about what we try to prevent.

However, if we imagine the ways we can achieve what we desire, and envision the feelings associated with those outcomes, our thoughts will be transported back from the Future Room to the Present Room, to allow us to experience what we've imagined to be true.

So if you're not achieving all you desire and wish you could go back in time to change what you've done—you can. Simply go into the Future Room, imagine what you want to achieve, and then look back at the past—which, from the future, means returning to the present. From here, you can now do what is necessary to achieve what you already imagined in the future; for in the future, yesterday is today.

THE STRESS TEST

Stress tests are a critical tool for gauging our physical health. Doctors use them to test our heart rate and blood flow because the physical exercise reduces tension in the body by increasing our blood flow. But what about mental health? When our thoughts are lost in the Future Room, worrying about what might happen, we experience emotional stress. Stress is a physiologic reaction to the accumulation of thoughts we can't get away from because we're not aware that we are in the wrong room.

Monitoring where our thoughts are is just as important as exercising our bodies. Both activities can reduce stress. By monitoring our thoughts, we can recognize factors that cause anxiety and tension in our lives, which ultimately affects our physical bodies. To learn how much stress really affects us, just ask the experts. Dr. Joe Dispenza, in his book *You Are the Placebo*, explains how long-term stress can do real physical damage. He writes, "Between remembering stressful experiences from the past and anticipating stressful situations coming up in your future, all these repetitive short-term stresses blur together into long-term stress." He goes on to say that, "No organism in nature is designed to withstand the effects of long-term stress.[1]"

Most people don't understand stress can do this kind of harm to their bodies because they don't realize how much stress they're creating in the first place. Obviously, the more stress you're experiencing, the more urgently you need to reduce it. Becoming aware of when your thoughts are in the Future Room is a good start, as those are the thoughts that typically produce the most stress. Monitoring your thoughts and physical exercise have the same results—you experience less stress. It's like a financial balance sheet. If you want to generate net income, you can either increase your gross income or you can lower your expenses. Either way will get you there, but the optimal path is to do some of both. Your most effective battle against stress should also include a bit of physical exercise *and* monitoring your thoughts.

Who feels the most stress? According to the American Psychological Association's 2016 annual "Stress in America" survey, the Millennial generation is now the most stressed-out generation. That might shock many, but it makes sense. Every generation yearns to be better than the generation before them. But there is no "better," just "different," and Millennials are certainly different from preceding generations. In many ways, this generation was born into a technological revolution much like that of the Industrial Revolution. The benefits of modern technology are staggering, and they give great power to those who use it. But as Uncle Ben Parker said in the *Spider-Man* movie, "With great power comes great responsibility."[2] The question is, are we using this power responsibly? Just look at social media. On one hand, it offers significant advantages, such as the ability to mass-communicate with people during crises. On the other hand, the amount of privacy we relinquish in the process brings back memories of Big Brother in George Orwell's futuristic novel *1984*.

We of the Baby Boomer generation had to deal with quite a few upheavals through the years as we tried to move our country away from war, racial segregation, gender discrimination, and rampant consumerism and toward peace, love, and Earth-embracing lifestyles. Many people from our generation expanded our hearts and minds but never fully let go of the material world either. Baby Boomers had glimpses of our connection to all living things, but because we live in the material world, we tend to focus on our differences. Still, it appears that we've managed to pass down glimpses of our Higher Selves and our oneness with all living things to the next generation—but also our attachment to material things, which continues to breathe life into the illusion of separation that keeps us separated.

Now Millennials must ask themselves, "What are we going to teach the next generation? Are we going to teach them that they live in a material world or that they are powerful on the inside?" The answer depends on what they believe is the causal level of this world: separation or oneness. What they need to decide is how they see the world, because that is the vision they will pass on to the next generation.

Fortunately, there are Millennials like Gabrielle Bernstein who have faced challenges and come out stronger because of them, and then shared their experiences. In her book *Spirit Junkie: A Radical Road to Discovery, Self-Love and Miracles*, she writes, "I've learned that fear is simply an illusion based on past experiences that we project into the present and on to the future."[3]

Daniel Chidiac is another gifted spiritual author who is inspiring a whole generation of young people. His book titled *WHO SAYS YOU CAN'T? YOU DO* is filled with deep insights and practical wisdom. When expressing the importance of the present moment, he states, "The 'past' is only a mental image, just as the 'future' is; however, they are pictures that affect how we act in the present."[4] As we move our thoughts out of the fear-based Future Room, we move closer to the loving environment of the Present Room.

At this moment, certain cultures understand the need to

focus on love rather than fear, while others don't. From one view, we can see fighting and violence in many parts of the world, with people killing each other in the name of God. From another view, we see love and compassion in other areas. Look no further than indigenous people throughout the planet like the Hopi, a Native American tribe, who has passed on a reverence for all living things to each successive generation. They seem to show none of the attachment to the material world that other cultures have. Wouldn't it be great if Millennials could feel that way right now?

THE UNDERDOG GENERATION

Everyone loves it when an underdog wins. Their victories are thrilling. In New York, we cheered wildly when the Giants beat the heavily favored Patriots in the Super Bowl—twice.

These types of outcomes are unexpected. They rarely happen because most underdogs listen to the rhetoric about how they have no chance of winning, and they accept it. They may say, "We're going to give it our best shot" or "We hope to make a game of it," but few people come out and say, "I don't care what the odds are. We are going to win this game." Joe Namath said something similar before the 1969 Super Bowl when no one thought the AFC Champions could beat the heavily favored Baltimore Colts in Super Bowl III. And Namath was proven right. Why do stories like these make us feel so good? It seems to be that the teams didn't believe that they weren't supposed to win. When they believe in themselves and beat the odds, it shows us that we can too.

In every case of a major upset, if the underdogs had believed what everyone else said—that they were not good enough—they never would have been able to pull off a victory. But they focused on two ideas: (1) It doesn't matter what everyone else thinks, and (2) anything is possible.

Right now, Millennials must feel like underdogs losing the battle because they came into the game late, and the generations before had a huge lead and then squandered it. The Baby Boomers had social triumphs (civil rights, feminism), astonishing innovations (space travel, computer technology), and prosperity. Now we have underfunded pension plans, a diluted Social Security system, and an aging population ill-prepared for retirement. As the number of people retiring grows, it is not surprising that both Generation X and Millennials feel the stress of supporting a massive retirement system with substantially fewer workers, not to mention other concerns such as their own job prospects and punishing student debt. Consequently, they spend a lot of time in the Future Room worrying about how their lives will unfold.

Stress is starting to affect Generation Z, as well. When I was in kindergarten, we mostly played with toys and blocks. Now children are pressured to learn to read and write in preschool, yet the United States is still falling behind other nations in academic standing. You hear stories of third-graders becoming more and more anxious as ever-increasing expectations are put on them. If adults and young adults have such difficulty managing stress, how are elementary school children expected to handle the increased stress in their lives? How do they even recognize it? They are spending more and more of their precious childhoods in the Future Room, and they don't even realize it.

As long as our thoughts remain in the Future Room, we will continue to experience stress. Stepping back and observing our thoughts creates the conscious awareness we need to transform the experience of stress into a feeling of peace. That act of observation helps us achieve this by slowing down the negative thought process about our stressful experiences in the external world and shifting our thoughts to the quiet peacefulness of our inner world. Until that shift takes place, stress remains our most unwanted companion.

ANXIETY ATTACKS

If you've never had an anxiety attack, you can't fully appreciate how debilitating it can be. During one, anxiety physically attacks your body by constricting the flow of blood to your heart. This is why panic attacks are often confused with heart attacks. Millions of people suffer from anxiety attacks each year. What brings on this condition?

Anxiety attacks develop from feelings of stress, and the most common place you will feel that way is in the Future Room. To be anxious means to experience uneasiness or worry, typically about something with an uncertain outcome. So you are not thinking about something that has already happened but something you think *might* happen. When your thoughts focus on what might go wrong in the future, you begin the process of internalizing the negative emotions that accompany anxiety. Some people question whether anxiety attacks are real or "just in your head." But what's the difference? The same part of the brain feels both physical and emotional pain, so anxiety attacks are physically and emotionally debilitating.

To stop these attacks, you need to address the root cause,

which is what you are thinking. We need to observe our thoughts. When we recognize they are stuck in the Future Room, they begin to loosen their grip on us. Gradually, we can let them go and slide back into the Present Room. Once we return to the Present Room, anxiety can no longer affect us. Just as darkness cannot coexist with light, anxiety—which is rooted in fear—cannot coexist with the love in the Present Room.

If the grip of anxiety feels too strong and you can't pull your thoughts out of the Future Room, try replacing anxiety with hope. Hope is the antidote for anxiety. Hope is the anti-stress medicine. Hope brings peace. It is the power of looking at something in the Future Room and bringing it into the Present Room.

In the movie *The Hunger Games*, Donald Sutherland's character conveys the power of hope when he states, "Hope. It is the only thing stronger than fear."[5] Although hope trumps fear, it is one of the most misused words in the English language. When people get stuck in the Future Room, they say things like, "I hope I don't fail that test" or "I hope it doesn't rain on my graduation day." But they're not really expressing the concept of hope; rather, they are using the word to mask feelings of insecurity. The real power of hope doesn't come from worrying about something in the future, but from visualizing a desired outcome and then bringing that vision into the present.

DON'T WORRY, BE HAPPY

In 1986, Bobby McFerrin released "Don't Worry, Be Happy."[6] The song became an immediate hit because it struck a chord in us all. While most people want to incorporate this message into their daily lives, many dismiss it as not being possible, as if the only people who can relax are those who live on a tropical island. "Surely my life is too complicated for that to be possible," they think, and they go on worrying about everything in their lives. They don't realize that worrying about the future puts them squarely in the Future Room, while the happiness they long for but think is out of reach waits for them in the Present Room. Bob Marley's classic song "Everything's Gonna Be Alright" expresses optimism and hope.[7] He's telling us to switch rooms, because optimists spend their time in the Present Room, while pessimists are stuck in the Future Room.

I find it puzzling that everyone knows the definition of optimist and pessimist, yet there are as many pessimists as optimists in the world—and that is being very generous to the optimists. Many say the world is dominated by pessimistic thinking, but I have never once heard anyone say, "I am a pessimist and I'm proud of it!" or "When I grow up, I want to be a pessimist." Nobody wants to be a pessimist! Nobody wants to admit they *are* a pessimist. So why are so many people pessimistic? That's the $64,000 question. You may actually consider yourself optimistic, while your friends and family may have a different opinion.

Pessimists are stuck in the Future Room. They worry about what might happen and always expect the worst. They drag others, and themselves, down. It's not fun to be around someone who always expects the worst. But when your thoughts are deep in the Future Room, you're not aware of your own thinking.

Optimists, on the other hand, are enjoyable to be around. But optimists seem to get more flak from other people than pessimists. People make fun of optimists. They call them Pollyannas.

Other people—especially pessimists—say optimists are living in a dream world. To a pessimist, there is nothing more annoying than an optimist. The optimist is annoying because the pessimist is listening to the ego and the optimist is listening to the Higher Self. The last thing the ego ever wants to do is give credit or recognition to the Holy Spirit.

In his book *Perfect Happiness*, spiritual author Jon Mundy shares the following quote from *A Course in Miracles*: "Happiness is your nature. It is not wrong to desire it. What is wrong is seeking it outside when it is inside."[8] In other words, we don't need to search for happiness outside of us. Truly happy people enjoy their lives; they live their lives "in joy," regardless of what is going on around them in the world of form.

My friend Steve Frosch was one of those people. Whenever you talked to Steve, you had his undivided attention. He always listened as if he cared, because he did, and he always smiled. The effect on other people was transformative. When his life tragically ended too early, the impact on those around him was profound. Of the thousand people who showed up to honor him, many talked about the special aura he had. Everyone felt drawn to him. What did Steve possess that others don't? Nothing. He just didn't possess the other stuff that many of us carry around, like judgment, prejudice, and pessimism.

At his memorial service, a family friend read a wonderful poem that reflected Steve's life. It was "The Dash," by Linda Ellis.[9] It is an inspiring poem that leads you to think about your life and how others will remember you when you leave this physical experience, or the time that you have between your birth and death (otherwise seen as a "dash" on a headstone). Steve didn't waste his dash, or his time on Earth. He inspired others to improve their dashes as well, in the way he lived his life. The one given regarding our time on Earth is that we all have a birth date and a death date. What is not certain is how we will spend the time in between. We should all spend our dash a little more the way Steve Frosch did, before we meet up with him again. For as Juba says at the end of the movie *Gladiator*, "I will see you again, my friend, but just not yet. Not yet."[10]

MY STUFF

When my sons, Brendan and Paul, were still young, I used a combination of real-life and made-up stories to teach them life lessons. One of my favorite fictional tales was "The King and the Pea," about a king obsessed with his wealth. While all the desperately poor people in his kingdom suffered, the king hoarded treasures in his castle. But that wasn't enough. He also wanted to make sure he could bring all his riches with him to Heaven. One day he heard about a guru who might be able to help him do this. He summoned the guru to his castle. When he arrived, the king told him of his desire to bring all his gold and treasures into Heaven. The wise man handed the king a single pea and said, "All you need to do is take this little pea with you into Heaven when you die, and all your treasures are sure to follow."

"That's great!" said the king, and he kept beaming until the guru was led out of the castle. Then he thought about what he'd said, and it dawned on him, "How am I supposed to take this pea with me to Heaven if I don't have a body anymore?" The king immediately ran after the guru and caught up with him about a mile down the road. "Excuse me, oh wise man, but I have one more question. How am I supposed to get this pea into Heaven with me?" The wise man looked at the king with loving eyes and said, "If you can't get that little pea into Heaven, how do you expect to get all those treasures in?" At that moment, the king realized he couldn't physically take anything with him to Heaven. From that point on, he began to share his wealth with all the people of the kingdom.

It is amazing how much stuff we accumulate in the material world. Even when we're not accumulating as much as we'd like, we're dreaming about how to get more. We think, "If only I were rich, I would buy this and that." But there is an important distinction between having stuff and attaching ourselves to these material possessions, between enjoying our stuff and acquiring a false sense of superiority because of it. If we go out and buy something because it makes us feel good inside, then great. Material things are good as long as they put a smile on our face when we're alone and not just when we show them off to the world. If we buy an object for the satisfaction of having others see us with it, then we're buying it for all the wrong reasons. We either learn to recognize things for what they are, or we identify with them and how they make us look to others. When our thoughts are in the Future Room, we focus on the latter.

Other people may be impressed with your stuff, but your Higher Self is not impressed at all. For your Higher Self, less is more. It wants to know what you are doing with the material things you already have, rather than how much more you can acquire. Doesn't it make more sense to acquire things you can keep forever, instead of things that will fade away? You can have all the power and money in the world, but the physical things that you acquire, you cannot keep forever. The king, like so many others, wanted to reach Heaven but couldn't let go of his physical possessions. He didn't understand that you need "no stuff" to reach nirvana, or, as Wayne Teasdale explains in his book *The Mystic Heart*: "The summit of contemplation, of the spiritual journey in the Buddhist understanding, is also the arrival into nirvana and nirvanic awareness. Nirvana is life and being beyond bondage to our desires. We only begin to see when we are free of desire, or craving. Our grasping for the objects of desire blinds us to the real. Nirvana sets us free, and allows us to develop wisdom."[11]

In the Future Room, we can't appreciate what we have because we are so preoccupied with what we don't have. But in reality, we already have everything we need and everything we can take with us when we leave the world of form.

THE NEEDY VS. THE GREEDY

For more than fifteen years, my family vacationed on the Outer Banks of North Carolina with friends. Each year, I would use the trip from Long Island to Nags Head as an opportunity to listen to audio tapes of spiritual teachers Marianne Williamson and Wayne Dyer, among others. By the time I reached my destination, I was already pretty relaxed. One of the most enjoyable aspects of those summer vacations was sitting under the stars at night and talking about life. I remember so well my friend John Nitti talking about the brilliant psychologist Abraham Maslow. "What a man can be, he must be" was John's favorite Maslow saying.[12] It quickly became my favorite as well, but there is more to Maslow than this one quote.

In 1943, Maslow wrote a paper titled "A Theory of Human Motivation," in which he first described his famous hierarchy of needs.[13] He looked at the characteristics of all high-achieving individuals and then created a road map for achieving self-actualization based on those needs. The self-fulfillment that he describes at the top of the hierarchy is akin to the alignment you can achieve with your Higher Self in the Present Room.

While Maslow focused on the importance of human needs, we generally have a different view of "needy" individuals. One type of needy person may not feel they lack anything, but society has compassion for them because they have fewer material goods than most others. We have food and clothing drives to help the "needy," which they really appreciate, but when they are centered in the Present Room, they don't need things to feel complete.

Then there is the other kind of "needy" person, who believes they lack a lot of stuff because they are focused on what everyone else has. In a sense, they are not "needy" so much as "greedy." It doesn't matter how much stuff they already have; it's never enough. They may "need" to buy a second fur coat because their friend has three of them. They *act* needy, but society has little compassion for them. The irony is that they spend their days in the Future Room focused on what they don't have, when all their physical needs are already met. Self-actualization waits for them in the Present Room.

"I Can" People vs.
"I Can't" People

The more time we spend in the Future Room, the more time we spend with our fears—the ones we have created. Here, we are afraid of what might happen to us, whether it is the result of our own actions, other people's actions, or even natural disasters. One of our deepest fears is the fear of failure. "What if I don't get that new job?" "What if I don't make the team?" When fear takes over, the thought of not getting that job becomes a devastating blow. If you don't make the team, you feel certain you will be chided and ridiculed. The fear of failure puts more pressure on what you are trying to achieve. Consequently, that self-inflicted fear can prevent you from achieving those things to which you aspire. It all comes down to love or fear. Love says, "I can." Fear says, "I can't."

Henry Ford once said, "Whether you think you can or you think you can't—you're right."[14] What we believe becomes our truth. If we believe we can do something, we have a feeling of confidence, which is self-love. If we believe we can't do something, we have a feeling of timidity, which is fearful and hesitant. Therefore, two statements, "I can" or "I can't," make all the difference between whether we feel love or fear. If we say, "I can" and feel the confidence of our self-love, we move into the Present Room. If we say, "I can't," we feel the fear of doubt and failure and move into the Future Room. Stress and anxiety then become our closest companions.

So, if you have the choice of saying, "I can," why would you ever say, "I can't"?

"YOU CAN" PEOPLE VS. "YOU CAN'T" PEOPLE

We can only be defined by what we think and say about ourselves. We cannot be defined by what other people say about us unless we allow it. When we listen to what other people tell us we can do, we start to doubt ourselves. It chips away at our self-confidence, and we succumb to the statement "I can't." But if we get to know who we really are inside, we won't be influenced by how others try to define us. As Wayne Dyer stated in *The Power of Intention*, "When doubt is banished, abundance flourishes, and anything is possible."[15] If this were easy, no one would ever doubt themselves again. But when our thoughts are in the Future Room, we think of all the things that could go wrong and end up doubting our ability to achieve our goals. Hence, we begin to use the words "I can't."

While "I can't" is understandable, "You can't" is inexcusable. If you want to deny yourself access to universal consciousness, that's your choice. But it is reprehensible to pass your negativity and naïveté on to someone else. It's wrong to use the negative power of "I can't" against others. When you say, "You can't do that," you increase the likelihood of that person saying, "I can't" to themselves.

Unless you are honestly trying to help or protect them, how do you benefit from telling someone else, "You can't"? Does it somehow make you feel better? The only logical explanation is that you feel *you* "can't," so you don't want someone else to believe they can. You try to pass your insecurities and doubt on to other people. It sounds foolish that this act of cowardice would ever succeed, but it often does. When the other person focuses their thoughts in the Future Room, they are susceptible to the fears others are trying to pass on to them. When you say, "You can't" to someone, you attack their self-esteem. You erode their self-confidence by making them feel less than they are. It feels like a challenge to their dignity.

Dignity is synonymous with self-esteem. Both are predicated on how we feel about ourselves, but too often we link them with how others treat us. If people put us down, our self-esteem takes a big hit. If they don't treat us with respect, we feel as if we are losing our dignity. But we don't have to allow other people's behavior to affect how we feel about ourselves.

In the movie *Glory Road*, during an emotional team meeting, one of the players tells the coach, "They are trying to take our dignity away from us." The coach, played by Josh Lucas, responds, "Your dignity is inside you. Nobody can take something away from you that you don't give them."[16] Truer words have never been spoken. People may say we can't do something, or we aren't good enough, but they can't take away our dignity because that comes from inside, and they can't touch that if we don't let them.

Other words that have a profoundly negative effect on us are "not enough." "You're not good enough." "You're not tall enough." "You're not pretty enough." But how do we define "enough"? The dictionary defines it as "adequate" and "sufficient." So, if someone tells us we are not enough, they are saying we are inadequate and deficient. No wonder those words break down our self-esteem and confidence and can lead to depression. They remove us from the loving environment of the Present Room and lock us into the fear-based mentality of the Future Room. We begin to believe the words "you can't" and "you are not enough." Some people with eroding self-esteem and deep-seated feelings of depression finally get to the point where they see no way out. That is a place that no one should ever reach.

TURNING THE TIDE: YOU CAN

It is hard to fathom that there are approximately one million people who commit suicide each year worldwide,[17] largely because they have come to believe they are not "enough." Isn't it time we did something about that? Let's start with a modest goal. Let's make that number 999,999. If we can do that, let's shoot for 999,998. One at a time. Every time you tell someone, "You can" or "You are enough," you can help knock that number down another digit. Every time you tell someone, "You can't" or "You are not enough," you have just potentially increased that number. It's up to you. It's up to *all of us*. Send the message "You can." Send the message "You are enough." Send it loud and send it clear!

If you want to change someone's life for the better, tell them, "Yes, you can." "You can become a doctor." "You can become an astronaut." "You can make the cheerleading squad." "You can be happy." If you hear someone else telling someone they "can't," step right in and correct them. Tell that person, "Of course you can!" "Of course you're good enough." It takes a village. When someone gets knocked down, help pick them up.

When my son Paul was in elementary school, he came home one day with a report on Dr. Martin Luther King Jr. We ended up discussing how King stood up for others when he could have just sat by and watched them be treated unfairly. We talked about the importance of standing up for others when they can't defend themselves. About a week later, Paul came home and said he was in the schoolyard when he saw a group of boys picking on another boy. Instead of watching like all the other kids who gathered around, Paul stepped in and helped defend the boy being picked on. It's the only time I ever recall Paul getting in a fight at school, and it was to stand up for someone who needed help. I could tell that made him feel good about himself, but that pales in comparison to how good the other boy must have felt when someone stepped in to help him. Someone's actions said, "You are worth defending, and you deserve to be treated right." Someone's actions said, "You are enough."

If you are that boy being picked on, or if people are always telling you that you are not enough, my question to you is: When are you going to say, "I've had enough of the negativity other people are trying to dump on me—enough of people who don't have a clue who I am trying to tell me what I can do"? When have you had enough? The answer is: right now. Transcend the ego. Remember that you share the same Divine consciousness as every spiritual master who has ever walked the face of the Earth. That is enough. *You* are enough.

CHAPTER 4

THE PRESENT ROOM

"YOU ARE ALWAYS PRESENT" IS ONE OF THE BEST COMPLI-ments that someone can give you. It means you are here, right now. It means you not only show up for work or appointments but show up for life. When you are with people, you're fully engaged. Your thoughts are not back in the Past Room or ahead in the Future Room. They are here, now. You're not talking to people while texting on your mobile device. You're not sitting in meetings while checking emails. You are fully present.

Being present means much more, as well. Being present means you can feel the vibrational frequency of the Divine within you, and you allow it to flow through you. You have no thoughts that attract negative emotions into your being. Nothing you see or hear can affect the spiritual energy you feel deep inside.

THE PRESENT IS THE MIDDLE ROOM

Being present is not predicated on where your body is in regard to location. You can be somewhere physically, but that doesn't mean you are *present*. We find examples all the time of people who aren't present in the moment. You may be watching a football game, for example, and the announcer says the quarterback "never showed up for the game." He's there physically, but he's not focused on the game he's playing.

What keeps us from being in the Present Room is our habit of looking into the Past Room, at who we once were—and of projecting that image into the Future Room, to who we might become—while failing to recognize that only in the Present Room are we who we really are. The person we were in the past is not who we are now. Even just on a material level, our physical bodies are constantly changing; the body of the past no longer exists. And the future is a mythical place we can never experience because when it finally gets here, it is no longer the future.

The present sits between the past and the future, and it is the only place we can feel our alignment with our eternal being. That is why the Present Room is the middle of the Three Rooms. There are no regrets of the past. There are no fears of the future. There is only an awareness of right now. The Present Room is the middle room. The Present Room is the *Tao*. The Present Room is The Way.

It is here in the Present Room that we find qualities like joy, peace, acceptance, and compassion. But most of all, we find love. Since most of us have experienced the unmistakable feelings of love, peace, and joy at some point in our lives, we usually know what we're looking for. Unfortunately, we don't always find them because our thoughts spend too much time in the wrong rooms.

Acceptance, on the other hand, we are less likely to experience. We seem to consider acceptance a sign of weakness. Our attitude tends to be "This is my life. I have to accept it." But acceptance doesn't mean we have to resign our lives to smallness.

ACCEPTANCE AND CHANGE

Acceptance simply means non-judgment. When we can accept things as they are, we are not judging them. Acceptance means accepting all parts of ourselves, too, warts and all. We try so hard to distance ourselves from our shortcomings, but they are our greatest teachers. As Alexander Pope says, "To err is human,"[1] and that's okay. Accept that you will make mistakes, but at the same time, accept that you are connected to the perfection of the Divine.

What we seem to have the most trouble accepting is where we are in life, if we're not where we think we should be. That's when we say things like, "I'll be happy when I get that promotion." We feel we can't accept the present moment because this is not where we *want* to be. But where we are right now is always exactly where we are *supposed* to be, whether we realize it or not. Spiritual teacher Iyanla Vanzant refers to the place we are now versus the place we want to be as being "in the meantime."[2]

There is never wasted time in your life. If you are not right where you think you want to be, consider yourself in the meantime. This is the place where you can clean house and straighten out your life, but it is not where you have to be miserable. It's where you need to picture what you would like to do with your life and then envision it as if it is already a reality. This is how acceptance leads to change.

Focus on how envisioning your future makes you feel, and you will automatically and subconsciously begin to do what you need to make it manifest. The meantime can be one of the most productive times in your life, as long as you recognize that the meantime is still the present. Acceptance of the meantime allows you to continue to feel the love of the Present Room, which can help you start to attract what you desire.

COMPASSION

Compassion is another greatly misunderstood emotion. We all like to think we're compassionate, but are we really? Most people believe they are "compassionate" because they feel compassion for certain people. But feeling compassion for some people and not for others is still making judgments.

True compassion depends on which voice we are listening to: the ego or the Holy Spirit. When we listen to the ego, it leads us to love some people and not others due to our belief in separation and, therefore, our propensity to make judgments. When we listen to the Holy Spirit, it leads us to love all people due to our belief in the Divine connection we all share. With the Holy Spirit as our guide, there is an absence of judgment. This is what compassion is all about. True compassion is feeling love for all. No exceptions.

There is no greater emotion than compassion. It is love on steroids. You can only achieve true compassion when you recognize your oneness with all other beings. But compassion is more than just love:

Compassion = Empathy + Joy

Empathy is for the suffering or unease that another human being is experiencing. We recognize that we all go through our own trials and tribulations and that someone else's experiences may be different from ours. *Joy* comes from the realization that these are just temporary bodies we are inhabiting until we all return to our eternal beingness.

In the Present Room, you allow your inner being to recognize the inner being in others, even if they can't recognize it themselves. In this deep recognition, there is no one to compare yourself or others to. There is no one to judge. There is only compassion, a love for all—a unity.

EVOLVING NEEDS

When we move into the Present Room, we don't transcend our desire to want things. In fact, our cravings for things to satisfy us increases. What changes is the *type of satisfaction* we crave. Our longing for cars, clothes, toys, and gadgets, as in the Future Room, feels less important to us as we develop an ever-growing desire for things that can never break or wear out or perish—the things we can take with us when we leave the physical world, like self-knowledge, wisdom, compassion, and love. When we discover these, we also experience a profound sense of gratitude. That is what is missing in the Future Room. That is what lives in the Present Room: gratitude for all.

The Present Room is where the future can be experienced now. When you envision something in the future, you need to assume it has already happened in order for it to manifest in your future physical reality. In the Present Room, you can experience the joy of achieving that which you desire before it actually manifests, because it's where you have already imagined it to be true. The lack of acceptance of an optimistic future is the biggest hindrance to people realizing their most personal desires, because they focus on the absence of what they desire instead of the feeling of the desire already fulfilled. They spend so much time in the Future Room believing they are planning for the future, but they can't bring that desire into their future reality until they move back into the Present Room and understand that the future state is actually created in the present.

Typically, we focus on what we think will make us feel good in the future instead of just feeling good right now. We say and do whatever we think will make us happy. But other people keep saying and doing things that make us unhappy. If we move into the Present Room, other people's behavior doesn't matter. When we're in the Past or Future Room, our thoughts start with what we see and hear, which in turn produces the emotions we feel. When we are in the Present Room, we start with the emotions we feel—predominantly love, joy, and compassion—and then use those feelings to create what we see.

LOSE THE "I"—FOCUS INWARD

All great spiritual teachings tell us the path to joy, happiness, and eternal bliss begins by looking within. Happiness is not "out there"; we can't find it in material possessions, controlling people, or trying to achieve social status. That is all just *maya*, illusion! In the Hindu tradition, deep contemplation is required to understand the feelings of Brahman. The concept of *saccidananda* is described as the infinite bliss of being infinitely aware of being. While we all would like to experience a bit of that, we don't take the time to look within because we are too busy looking without. We are so dependent on waking up in the morning and drinking our coffee to get us going. If you really want to give yourself a jolt, wake up and say, "Give me two shots of *sacci*." That will get you going!

The Buddhists, meanwhile, tell us *nirvana* is achieved by letting go of things "out there" and becoming aware of all the things "in here." The only difference between "there" and "here" is the "t"—so remove it! When your thoughts are out *there*, focusing on what you see and hear in the world of form, you are being pulled into the Past or Future Room. Conversely, *here* is now, in the present, and when you are here, you are living in the Present Room. It's your choice. "There" or "here"? Lose the "t."

The Bible says, "The kingdom of God is within you" (Luke 17:21).[3] Can it be any clearer than that? The Bible not only tells us we all have access to the kingdom of Heaven but also tells us exactly where to find it—inside ourselves! When we look within, we can see we are all connected to the same Divine consciousness. We cannot look out into the physical world and make sense of someone telling us we are all one. Our eyes tell us differently. We are convinced we are all separate based on what we see, and we go through life noticing our supposed differences. Then, our ego takes those differences and turns them into judgments. When this happens, you see yourself not only as different from another person but also as better or worse than them. Even if you think others are better than you, the ego will start to pick them apart and find cracks in their armor. "Yeah, he may be a good-looking guy, but he's a real jerk." "Yes, she may be thinner than me, but she's not very nice." We can't help these kind of thoughts, and we don't even realize we are thinking them.

The more you look within, the more you will feel connected to those around you and thus feel the power of love. If you can't feel it inside, you will never find it outside. But once you *do* feel it inside, you will start to see it and feel it wherever you go in the physical world. There are so many amazing people on this planet filled with love and compassion. They have messages of hope that can fill your heart with joy. The best part is you have access to them all. All you have to do is step into the Present Room and feel the love in your heart. With this shift in awareness, you will be drawn to inspiring people across the world. You may find them on the street, through a friend, or via the internet. It doesn't matter. You'll hear their message, feel their love, and allow their light to shine through you.

DIG DEEPER, EVEN WHEN IT GETS HARD

Although you can find inspiring messages everywhere you look, your focus should continue to be directed inward. The famous Jules Verne novel *Journey to the Center of the Earth* serves as a powerful metaphor for the spiritual journey inside ourselves.[4]

Verne's characters aren't just traveling; they are working their way deeper and deeper inside the Earth, and the farther they go, the more obstacles they encounter. Your spiritual journey will be similar. The further you go inside, the tougher the obstacles become. This is because the ego doesn't want you to get there. The ego doesn't want to release its grip on you. When moments of light break through, you'll find them scary as hell. You'll want to back up. This is why the journey takes courage. It takes persistence. It takes determination. Keep working your way inside, to the center of your heart.

When you focus on the external world, you become prisoner to it. It dictates all your thoughts and actions. You can try to figure it out, but you can't possibly know all the variables necessary to achieve your goals. Sometimes things appear to be going well, and then they take a turn for the worse. You continuously react to what is going on in the external world. Sometimes you react appropriately and sometimes you don't, either because you lack information or because your emotions get the better of you. In either case, the dynamic you experience is action, reaction, action, reaction. When you focus on what is out there, you have no control over how events make you feel. You can only react to them. Only when you make a complete shift to viewing the world from within can you control how you feel, despite what is taking place on the outside. When your vision is focused inward, outside events don't affect your emotions in the same way. In the Present Room, your vision focuses inward. That's why in the Past and Future Rooms, you are affected by what you see transpiring in the outer world, but in the Present Room, you are able to affect what you see.

EVERY DAY IS HALLOWEEN

Once a year, on Halloween, we walk around knowing that people aren't really who they appear to be on the outside. For one day, we withhold our usual judgment. We don't look at people in costumes and masks and say, "There's Batman, he's a good guy" or "There's the Riddler, he's a bad guy." We recognize that their outer appearance does not reflect who they are inside. Likewise, if we wear a Halloween costume, we don't care what people say about our physical appearance because they don't know who we really are. They only see the external disguise, so we let any hurtful words pass over us.

Well, every day of your life should be similar. It doesn't matter what anyone says about your physical appearance, because they have no idea who you are inside. If every day were Halloween, we would view people differently, recognizing they're not really who they appear to be on the outside. We also wouldn't care what they thought about how we looked because our outer appearance says nothing about who we are within. Our bodies are just a costume.

I've always thought there was something intriguing about costumes and disguises. Think of fairytales or movies where there is a masquerade ball and nobody can tell who anyone else is, even if they're only wearing a small mask over their eyes. It's hard to believe Prince Charming can't recognize Cinderella until she puts on the glass slipper. Don't you feel like screaming, "Really, you can't tell who that person is?"

Kids seem to get the symbolism easily, which is one of the reasons they love Halloween. They get to dress up and pretend to be someone they're not. But don't we all do that every day of our lives? People can't see us for who we really are because all they see is this external body we walk around in, with this personality we have created based on who we want others to think we are.

The real question to ask yourself is: Do you see the differences between yourself and other people, or do you see the sameness?

Most people don't immediately perceive our oneness with others because it's not what they see with their eyes. We're so trained to look at the physical world and see our separateness from others that it is difficult to recognize the sameness. Picture a movie in which you and a small group of friends are battling an alien race for control of the planet. It is a mighty struggle, and you start to feel overwhelmed by the machines or monsters. Suddenly, you see another group of humans coming to assist you. You feel an immediate sense of relief, appreciation, and camaraderie with the members of that group. That's because you recognize your sameness with them as fellow humans, and you believe they will help fight off the invaders. It's easy for all of you to join together as one.

Now imagine another scenario. You are back in the movie with the other group of humans coming toward you, but this time you focus on their differences from you, instead of your sameness. You think, "What the heck are they wearing? Who are these guys? Where are they from, anyway? I'm not joining up with people from over there!" Now, your differences drive you apart and you start arguing. Before you know it, the aliens have destroyed you all.

It sounds comical that people would do this, but it's what we do every day. We don't recognize our oneness as a human race; instead, we focus on our separateness. But we have the choice to see our sameness and feel compassion for all. If we accepted that our bodies are just costumes, this kind of unity would be easier to attain. The sameness inside all of us is disguised by the differences in our appearances. Are you going to be fooled by the costume, or are you going to see through it? It's your choice. It's *our* choice.

COCOON

It doesn't take much to recognize that our bodies appear to be constantly changing. Every time we look in the mirror, we see minor differences. Every time we examine an old picture of ourselves, we see major changes. But the you who is aware of these changes in your body is changeless. Your Inner Self, the one that is aware of the changes, is infinite. The same is true of everybody else, too. Their bodies are constantly changing, but what's inside is not. If you are aware of this, you will know who they really are. They are eternal beings in a physical body—just like you.

In the 1985 movie *Cocoon*, Brian Dennehy plays an elder visiting from another planet.[5] An Earthling asks him about "forever," and he is somewhat perplexed by the question because he doesn't know what forever means. When you recognize that your true self is infinite, you have no need for the term "forever." In the movie, there's a poignant scene where Tahnee Welch plays another visitor from the same planet. Before going to bed, she literally peels off her physical body. As the light from within her bursts out, Steve Guttenberg's character happens to be watching and falls over in disbelief. Now think about the next morning when she had to put that suit back on. She was a being of light who had squeezed herself into a body suit to fit in with people on Earth. The symbolism is overpowering. If you want to hang out in the Present Room, you need to "shed your attachment to your body"; that is, you need to recognize that you are the perfect blending of the physical you and the non-physical you. When in that room, it's not that you don't see other people's bodies, you just don't identify with them.

You're a Firework

Every generation has its share of inspirational works and charismatic leaders, people who seem to transcend existing culture. Sometimes they are world leaders, like Winston Churchill and John F. Kennedy, and other times they are spiritual leaders, such as Mahatma Gandhi and Mother Teresa. Very often, such people are poets or writers. Artists have always played a major role in inspiring people to question the very fabric of society. Sometimes such inspiration comes from unexpected places.

In 1962, a young man from Minnesota by the name of Robert Zimmerman, a.k.a. Bob Dylan, wrote an anthem called "Blowin' in the Wind."[6] This song inspired my entire generation to search deep within our consciousness and question why we were allowing our nation to choose war over peace. More recently, another artist has implored her generation to look deep inside themselves when everything seems to be going wrong on the outside. In 2010, Katy Perry released the song "Firework,"[7] which essentially tells us to lose the "t" in "there." The solution to all our problems, she implies, is not out there but in here. She guides us to ignite the spark inside and let our light shine. There can be no better message for a generation of young people.

When your thoughts are in the wrong room, you can feel like you're trapped. The door is closed, and it looks as if there's no way out. You may not even realize you're in the wrong room, but the negative emotions you feel are undeniable. So open the door and follow the path right into the Present Room. Celebrate who you really are and not who other people think you are. Or, as Perry suggests, ignite the light inside—feel the power of love—and let it shine. Ultimately, this is not a song about the Fourth of July but an anthem for a generation.

The hit television show *Glee* delivered a similar message. This show taught us it's okay to be different on the outside, to not look and sound just like everyone else, and to stop pretending to be someone we're not. We may look different on the outside, so people make judgments about our clothes, our hair, our personalities. But we're not different on the inside.

You can find inspiration from artists like these, and they are all around you. They will help guide you back into the Present Room, where you will feel the power of love within you and love everyone else unconditionally.

DEVELOPMENT OF A KNOWING

The greatest gift we can receive is the experience of perfect alignment with our inner being. This is not to be confused with *believing* we are one with that eternal being. A lot of people believe in that connection, but that doesn't mean they truly understand it. You can believe in many things you don't absolutely *know* to be true. Your thoughts create a belief, but an experience creates a knowing. To experience something is to feel it. The only way to experience our Higher Self is to feel love. The only place to feel love is in the Present Room. Consequently, the only place to get to know our Higher Self is the Present Room.

I went through my own experience of complete "knowing" in the summer of 1997. I was a single dad at the time, and I imagined meeting someone new. I wasn't thinking about what she would look like but how I would feel when I met her. I hadn't been ready to meet someone earlier because I still had work to do on myself, trying to connect to my eternal being inside. Though I didn't realize it, I had finally gotten to the point where I was completely at peace with myself, and I became whole. I was ready to attract into my life someone who was also whole.

I found myself walking along the Long Beach, New York, boardwalk one summer day, and I had a powerful *knowing* that I would meet someone. I could feel myself being led by a force far greater than myself, a feeling in my heart. As I walked along the boardwalk, I kept asking myself, "Is that her? How about her?" I wondered when she would appear. Finally, when she didn't, I went down to the beach, lay down on my towel, and started to read a book.

It wasn't long before a large wave came up and nearly drenched my towel. I snatched it away, turned, and started back up the beach. I nearly walked straight into a woman sitting on a blanket, also reading a book. I stopped. She noticed the startled look on my face and said, "Hi, my name is Aimee." I felt an instant recognition that this was who I was supposed to meet. I introduced myself and asked if I could join her.

We would stay together for two years. During that time, she introduced me to the writings of Neale Donald Walsch. I remember her saying, "You need to read this. It's right up your alley." She was right. I devoured his *Conversations with God* trilogy, which only served to strengthen my relationship with my eternal being. Our Higher Self is always trying to guide us toward the people who will benefit us the most at that particular moment in our life. Too often, we let our thoughts get in the way of that guidance, which is always evolving with us. My relationship with Aimee set the stage for the more permanent one yet to come.

LIVING FEARLESSLY

We've all known fearless people. They are the ones who do things no one else can. They take risks. When I was growing up, my friend Tim Cannella was one of those guys. When we were teenagers, I saw him do a double-flip off a tree branch into a lake, not knowing if there were two or ten feet of water below him.

But physical bravado is only one kind of fearlessness. Being fearless also means not being afraid to stand up for what you believe in. Mahatma Gandhi was fearless. At the risk of being imprisoned, tortured, or worse, he stood up for a whole nation of people and taught them to "be truthful, gentle, and fearless." Dr. Martin Luther King Jr. was also fearless. Fulfilling a mission that ultimately took his life, he stood up for a whole race of people and taught them it was the love in their hearts and not the color of their skin that mattered.

To teach about peace, love, and acceptance, these leaders first had to feel it in their hearts. To feel it in their hearts, they had to be centered in the Present Room. That's where the love is. You will never find fear there because love and fear cannot coexist. If people like King and Gandhi had been stuck in the Past Room, their fear-based thoughts would have generated feelings of anger and revenge. If their thoughts had been in the Future Room, they would have been too afraid of the consequences of their actions and might never have inspired the countless people they did. Living fearlessly means feeling only love and compassion, despite what is going on around you. Being fearless means living in the Present Room.

ACCEPTING DEATH BY EMBRACING LOVE

If there is one thing that almost everyone is afraid of, it is dying. We are afraid of death because it is one of the great mysteries of life. It is the great unknown; anyone on this planet who is talking about it hasn't experienced it. Very often, the people who most fear death are those who most fear life. They spend most of their time in the Future Room, afraid of what other people think of them, afraid of what might happen to them here on Earth if things don't go as they planned. And, of course, they are scared to death . . . of death.

Being afraid of what comes after the end of our physical life is not surprising, because for many of us death evokes fearful images instead of positive ones. We may picture the Grim Reaper coming at us with a scythe instead of angels coming to gently scoop us up.

In 1990, the wonderful movie *Ghost* illustrated the perceived difference between a bad person's death and a good person's death.[8] When the deceitful character played by Tony Goldwyn gets killed, he is dragged away by a group of little Grim Reaper-looking demons. At the end of the movie, though, when it is time for the honest Patrick Swayze character to leave the physical plane, the heavens open and he is drawn to the light. As he goes, he says to the partner he leaves behind, "The love inside, you take it with you."

These different perspectives about the afterlife illustrate the importance of love. You take it with you because love is the same on Earth as it is in Heaven. This is why when you feel love, you experience "Heaven on Earth." When you feel love, you have nothing to fear. When you feel love, you don't have to go to the Present Room. You are already there.

Our bodies are finite. They can't last forever. When we shed our attachment to our bodies while we're still in this world, we catch a glimpse of what is to come: the feeling of pure love.

Typically, when you listen to stories of people who have had near-death experiences (NDEs), where their bodies physically died and then they were brought back to life, they describe feelings of great joy, love, and light. As inspirational speaker Anita Moorjani says in her memoir *Dying to Be Me*, "We are not these bodies; we're neither our accomplishments nor our possessions— we are all one with the Source of all being, which is God."[9]

Many survivors of NDEs report seeing a tunnel with a light at the end, drawing them near. They say that after they ascend this tunnel, they leave the world of form and embrace the light. They do not worry about anything that happened to them in the past, and they have no worries about the future. These people don't say, "Wait, I need to go to the dry cleaners first and pick up my clothes." They are drawn to the light, and they are at peace. People who have experienced NDEs also say that what we see here in our world is not real, nor is it all there is; there is something greater than what we perceive in the world of form. They know it because they felt it.

On the one hand, it is not surprising that people are most afraid of dying. On the other hand, you'd think we would be grateful to be free from all the fear we carry while here on Earth. It doesn't make sense to say, "No, no, don't bring me into the light of eternal peace and happiness. I'm too busy worrying about what other people think about me here on Earth." But it is understandable why some people may be afraid of leaving their loved ones behind, or just terrified of the uncertainty of death. Even so, they would be a lot more at peace if they could say, "I know I will physically die someday and will have to embrace it. But first, I will embrace life while I am here." There is only one place to embrace life and love: the Present Room.

THE PRESENT CLUB

Look around and you will find all kinds of discrimination. People tend to associate with people who are like them and exclude others they perceive to be different. Most people aren't even aware they discriminate so much, and they'll deny it if confronted. Groups and organizations all over the globe also discriminate against other groups, refusing to admit them into their "clubs." Some clubs exclude Jews, others exclude Christians or Muslims, and that's only religious discrimination. Other clubs reject people based on skin color, political views, sexual preference, gender, or economic status. But there is one club that admits anyone who wants to join: the Present Club. Membership is open to anyone who chooses to live in the Present Room.

Membership in the Present Club doesn't admit you to a rifle range, a golf course, a swimming pool, or a polo match. It simply provides you access to a world of love, bliss, and tranquility. The Present Club includes every mystic and enlightened master who ever walked the face of the Earth. When you live in the present moment, there is nothing and no one to discriminate against. You all share the same consciousness—and that is one of non-judgment.

Do I belong? That is a question we're always asking ourselves about any club. Too often, the ego (as well as other people) makes you feel like you don't belong. For whatever reason, in that group, you don't belong. When people tell you that you don't belong, they are saying you are not good enough. You are not one of them. You are different. Why would you want to be with these people? Stop trying to feel as though you belong where you don't really want to be. Follow the group that says you *do* belong, the Present Club.

It's unfortunate that our society has such a history of exclusion. The message is always the same: "You're not welcome here!" Children do it to other children in the schoolyard. We even do it to friends. One minute they're great, and the next minute they're no longer welcome. We've all experienced the feeling of exclusion, and it's uncomfortable, to say the least. It is a lonely feeling.

Exclusion is rooted in a belief in separation. Inclusion is rooted in a belief in unity. You will only find inclusion in the Present Club. That's because the Present Club is different from all other clubs. The Present Club says, "You're just like us. You just don't realize it yet. You're just like every spiritual master who ever existed. You share the same mind and the same consciousness with them because there is only one mind. It has many names, like Divine consciousness, Christ consciousness, and Buddha consciousness." When you step through the front door of the Present Club, all the enlightened masters who ever walked the Earth are there to greet you, as well as spiritually aligned people who are still living. Look for these welcoming people wherever you go.

The Past Club and the Future Club are the opposite. Members of those clubs cling to a thought system based on separation. They focus on how they are different from everyone else. If you want to experience drama, the Past and Future Clubs cling to belief in separation, are quick to judge, and are full of fear.

But there is a part of all of us that is not separate. When we finally remember this powerful fact, we can move back into the Present Room and join the Present Club. That's when we awaken. We awaken from the dream of separation to the consciousness of unity.

CHAPTER 5

MOVING FROM ROOM TO ROOM

ACCORDING TO GANDHI, THE PROBLEM WITH THE WORLD IS that we are not in our right minds. When viewed through the lens of the Three Rooms, we can reinterpret Ghandi as saying we are not in the right room, and we need to switch rooms.

When we talk about moving our thoughts from room to room, it means moving our focus from the Past and Future Rooms back into the Present Room. We shift our emotions from the fear-based rooms into the room that radiates love. Although this may sound difficult, you never have to worry about finding the Present Room. There is a part of you, your eternal being, that is always there. Your thoughts pull you away from the Present Room—away from your eternal being. So monitor your thoughts, and when they pull you into another room, notice them, acknowledge them, release them, and you will automatically rejoin your Higher Self in the Present Room. This realignment with our eternal being in the Present Room is one of our main purposes in life.

LEARN TO SEE THE EGO'S TRICKS

We're constantly getting pulled out of the Present Room by what we think, what we hear, and what we see. The hardest part of being taken out of the Present Room is becoming aware that you have left it. When you're pulled into the Past or Future Room, there are no signs announcing, "You are now out of the Present Room."

In fact, the ego will do everything possible to keep you from going back to the Present Room. What a surprise—that's the only room it can't hang out in. The ego's goal is to slip you into one of those other rooms without you realizing it.

The cleverest trick the ego uses to pull us out of the Present Room is our thoughts. They sneak into our minds like a stealth bomber in the middle of the night. We so rarely monitor our thoughts. One minute a thought pops into our minds, and it can immediately sweep us into a confluence of negative emotions triggered by memories of painful past experiences. Since the emotions we feel seem real, we get caught up in more thoughts that can fuel ever more negative emotions. In the blink of an eye, we've been pulled into the Past Room.

Words are another tool the ego uses to pull us out of the Present Room. No matter where we go, we can always hear people talk, and most of the time the words they are saying don't have much impact on how we feel. But when we hear words that remind us of an unpleasant experience, they take us right back to how we felt at that time in our past. Or, if we hear a word that reminds us of something we are anxious about, we are suddenly fearful of the future. Someone may speak to us directly, or we might overhear another conversation or hear something on television. It doesn't matter where the words come from; all that matters is whether we let them affect us.

Another common way we get yanked out of the Present Room by our ego is through what we see. Wherever we go, we are constantly looking at people, objects, and incidents despite what we're thinking or hearing. When we witness something, the ego is always ready to pounce on it and make assumptions or judgments about it. Because of our belief in separation, we perceive what we see as separate from ourselves. Therefore, we can't help but make judgments. As soon as we start to judge rather than observe, we've already left the Present Room.

AVOID GETTING STUCK IN THE WRONG ROOM

Most of our problems don't arise when we *move into* the Past or Future Room but when we *stay* there. We get so caught up in what we think about the past and future that we forget to live the life we envisioned for ourselves in the present. We're so worried about not missing out on some future something that we don't stop and feel the present moment. As John Lennon said, "Life is what happens while you're busy making other plans."[1]

Experiencing the fullness of life is not about never leaving the Present Room. It's simply about becoming aware that you have left and remembering what it felt like when you were there. This feeling is your reminder to go back. Still, you have to figure out how to get back once you leave.

Why do we want to get out of the Past and Future Rooms? Many people will make the argument that we need to learn from the past and plan for the future, so we can't always be in the present. That is not true. Being an observer of the past is quite different from being trapped in the Past Room. When your thoughts take you to the Past Room, you don't realize you're there, so any fearful memories can fill you with negative emotions. Of course, we can have pleasant memories, too, but they fill us with positive emotions and therefore don't pull us out of the loving environment of the Present Room. When you are in the Present Room and you look back on your past as an observer, you're not *driven* by any fear-based memories because you, the observer, are watching from the Present Room, where all your decisions, based in love, come from.

You can look in on the Past or Future Room while remaining in the Present Room, as long as you know where you are. If you're aware you're in the Present Room, you can visit the other rooms without losing your awareness of the present. Negative emotions only arise when you're not aware you're in the Past or Future Room. When your thoughts get stuck in the past, and any of the negative emotions associated with dwelling on the past start to consume your life, that's when you want to be able to get out of there.

Obviously, you need to monitor your thoughts to know which room you're in, but ironically, when you're in the Present

Room, you don't need to be thinking. Instead, your thoughts are transformed into an awareness of your Higher Self. What's significant here is not what you're thinking but what you're *not* thinking. You're *not* thinking about the past, you're *not* thinking about the future, you're simply aware of the present. *A Course in Miracles* teaches that we don't need to do anything to get love or go anywhere to find it. We simply need to remove all barriers to love's presence. The same concept applies to accessing the Present Room. Remove all the fear-based thoughts of the Past and Future Rooms and you'll become conscious of the love-based Present Room.

But *how* do you observe your thoughts? Just sit down and quietly wait for thoughts to come into your mind. As soon as you recognize a negative one, release it immediately. Imagine you think *I can't believe Sally said that last night; she is such a*— stop. Discard that thought. It's clearly from the wrong room. You sit in silence for a moment or two. Then, *I really need to go to the grocery store.* Okay, that's a useful thought. Put that on your to-do list. Next . . .

This is how you start to monitor your thoughts, by starting to observe where they come from and identifying how they make you feel. While you are doing this, without even realizing it, you're now separating your awareness from your thoughts. As you do this, you begin to associate yourself with your awareness rather than with possibly negative or harmful ideas. Once you do that, you realize you're moving into the Present Room.

We need to get out of the Past Room not just because it can bring about negative feelings, but because we tend to cling to things we learned in the past, even if they may be no longer true. Each generation holds on to ideas they were taught, reluctant to open their eyes to new evidence that those ideas no longer represent who we are. Modern science is constantly discovering new truths in the field that displace the old "truths." Or consider the Middle Ages, when people believed absolutely that the world was flat. If someone like Christopher Columbus had stayed in the Past Room, he never would have sailed for America because he would have been too afraid of falling off the edge of the world. Moving into the Present Room allows people to open up to the concept of a whole new potential world because they're able to leave their old ideas behind.

Humanity is undergoing a massive shift in consciousness, from a near-universal belief in separation to a growing belief in oneness, but we still have a long way to go. For this shift to occur, we need to understand what a consciousness of separation means. This concept has been hard for us to grasp. The Past and Future Rooms are simply aspects of a belief in separation, that is, a belief that the core being of others is different from our own and that we are affected by what others say and do. How do we change this belief? To change belief in separation, we need to change our thoughts by monitoring them. If they're in the Past or Future Room, they are, by definition, thoughts of separation. If they're in the Present Room, we will have transformed them into an awareness of oneness.

Humanity's shift in consciousness from its belief in separation to a belief in oneness is predicated on moving from one room to the other. Everyone should be able to understand this idea and do it.

SURRENDER YOUR GRIP ON THE PAST AND FUTURE

If you have been stuck in the Past or Future Room, one of your first steps out is to completely surrender to your Higher Power. Whether your life is a total mess or you just don't feel at peace, complete surrender is one of the quickest ways to change rooms. "Surrender" requires nothing more than sitting down and saying to yourself, "Okay, I'm finally willing to do it your way." When you say "your way," you are communicating with your Divine Source. When you say "my way," you're putting the ego in charge. Whoever you put in charge will dictate which room you're in.

It's not hard to let the ego take over your internal steering wheel because it never wants to let it go. It is the guest who never wants to leave your house, the intoxicated driver who won't give up the keys to his car. Unless you finally say to the ego, "Okay, buster, your time is up," you'll never change rooms. Complete surrender is not saying, "Okay, I give up on life." It is saying, "Okay, ego, I give up my faith in you. There's a new sheriff in town." If you are serious about changing rooms, you need to cut the ego loose and surrender to the Holy Spirit. Speak to your ego the way Michael Douglas talks to the senator played by Richard Dreyfuss in the movie *American President*: "This is a time for serious people, Bob, and your fifteen minutes are up."[2]

We're programmed to resist the concept of surrender. We buy into the spirit of Winston Churchill's famous words, "Never give in. Never give in. Never. Never. Never."[3] As a consequence, we associate the term "surrender" with quitting. To the ego, focused on the external world, surrendering *is* quitting. It seems to be relinquishing our power. In actuality, surrendering to our Higher Self is the most empowering thing we can do. If you really want to follow Churchill's advice, then never ever give up your faith in the Holy Spirit. Never ever give up your connection to the Divine. Never ever give up your commitment to moving into the Present Room.

Experiencing the serenity of the Present Room requires eliminating the ego's constant chatter in your head. Once you surrender to your Higher Power and inhabit the Present Room, your experience of life changes. Eckhart Tolle says in *The Power of Now*, "It is the quality of your consciousness at this moment that is the main determinant of what kind of future you will experience, so to surrender is the most important thing you can do to bring about positive change."[4] In other words, when you surrender, you immediately connect with the Divine consciousness we all share. Surrendering simply means shifting from chatter to awareness, which puts you right back in the Present Room.

Until you completely surrender to your Higher Power, it's hard to comprehend how powerful this Higher Power is. I've had my own experience of surrendering, and it wasn't because I was filled with loving thoughts. This took place in the summer of 1996, a year or so after I'd had my moment of reckoning with God while standing on my bed. I'd moved to an apartment near the beach, and I was still filled with anger. I had thoughts of resentment and revenge, and I couldn't get them out of my head. I was stuck in the Past Room and didn't know it. One day, sitting in my apartment, I couldn't take it anymore. I screamed out loud, "Okay, I give up! What do you want me to do?" Before I even understood what I'd said, I was pinned to the floor by an internal force greater than anything I'd felt before. One message kept running through my head as I lay on the floor: "Forgiveness. It's all about forgiveness."

In that moment, an indescribable feeling of relief washed over my body. All my tension seemed to fly right out of me. I was overcome with giddiness and laughter. "Okay," I said out loud. "I got it." The ensuing peace that enveloped me was transformative. All the negative emotions pent up inside me, which I'd been hiding from the world, were released. Once I surrendered, I finally found a way to defeat them. That was the power of forgiveness.

THE ORDER OF PRIORITIES

When you're on an airplane, why do they tell you to put your oxygen mask on before you put one on your child? You'd do anything for your child. You'd give your life for them. So, why give oxygen to yourself first? Isn't that the most selfish thing you could do? Not at all. You put your mask on first because you need to take care of yourself before you can take care of others. You need to take care of yourself *in order to* take care of others. There's an order of priorities. If you don't take care of yourself, you can't help your child or anyone else.

The same principle applies to all relationships in your life. This includes family, friends, work relationships, and all acquaintances that you have. Yes, that even includes your partner. For example, I consider my wife my soul mate. I can't imagine not sharing the rest of my life with her. Yet she is not my number-one priority in this lifetime. My number-one priority is aligning vibrationally with my Higher Self. Once I achieve that, my relationship with my wife will be better than I ever could have imagined and certainly far better than it ever would be if I were not aligned with my Higher Self. That is the same as putting God first. That is what all the mystics do. It is a never-ending quest to personally know that part of you that is connected to our Source.

Forgiveness works the same way: You need to forgive yourself before you can forgive others. If you can't forgive yourself, you cannot truly forgive others.

Sometimes we don't think we've done anything wrong, so we don't realize we need to forgive ourselves. But we can be unconsciously brutal to ourselves and full of guilt. Then when someone else harms us, we don't consider forgiving them. Instead, we look at them with scorn and plot our revenge. The unconscious dynamic is: *I can't forgive myself, so I am certainly not going to forgive that bastard.*

Forgiveness is based on your willingness to see someone's innocence rather than perceiving them as guilty. Too often we think, "I don't need to think about whether he is innocent. I know he did it and he's guilty as sin!" Even if you believe someone acted intentionally to harm you, their Inner Self, the part of them that is connected with you, is not at fault. If you can remember this, you will recognize the Divine Spirit in the person who harmed you, a Divine Spirit you both share. You'll understand that their ego temporarily grabbed the steering wheel from their eternal being and acted unkindly toward you. Perceiving someone as innocent doesn't mean they didn't do something in this physical world to harm you. It means you are aware that their actions were driven by the ego, which is controlled by their fear. Therefore, they were not in their "right mind." It can be easier to forgive them when you feel compassion for how they are overcome by their fears and doubts.

When you understand that someone is not in their right mind, you can see the innocence inside of them. However, if *you* are not in your right mind, you can only see what they did to you and judge them as guilty. You can't see their innocence because your ego knows only how to judge others.

Forgiveness does not depend on what others have done to you but rather on your state of mind. If you're stuck in the Past or Future Room, controlled by the ego's fearful thoughts, you can't fully forgive someone. Only if you move into the Present Room, guided by your Divine Spirit, will you be in your "right mind" and able to see someone else's innocence.

It has been said that to forgive is a selfish act. For many, the selfishness of forgiveness is a difficult concept to grasp. If we forgive someone, we feel as if we're letting them off the hook. But if we don't forgive them, we actually keep ourselves on the hook; we retain all the negative emotions we feel toward them that require forgiveness in the first place. Unless we renounce those negative emotions, they stay with us and cause us long-term physical and emotional harm. How do we release the negative energy that gets trapped in our hearts? We forgive. This is the key to freeing up the space to allow our spiritual energy to flow through us.

If you truly forgive from your heart, which is recognizing your oneness with the other person rather than your differences, negative energy disappears. Forgiveness is a release, and after all, isn't that what we are all trying to do? Release the bad feelings we are experiencing? Release the jealousy? Release the resentment? Release the negative energy we are holding on to? Those are the same negative emotions we feel in the Past and Future Rooms. Once released, we are free to move back into the Present Room.

DON'T EXPECT AN APOLOGY

One of the biggest stumbling blocks to forgiving others is our expectation of repentance. It's easier to forgive someone when they've said they're sorry. If someone doesn't apologize for what they did or said, we feel more justified in our non-forgiveness. *Screw him; he never even said he was sorry.* We tend to think that if we forgive someone, we're condoning what they did and have to keep the same relationship with them. But forgiving someone doesn't mean we still have to maintain the status quo. We can choose not to socialize with the person and still feel peaceful inside when we happen to be around them. But when we choose not to forgive someone, we can't feel peaceful inside, even when we're away from them.

Forgiveness is a choice, albeit a challenging one. Forgiveness is about our ability to see past someone's behavior. If their behavior is not loving, it doesn't represent who they really are. One of you needs to recognize that, and if their behavior continues to be unloving, it's not going to be them. Through complete forgiveness, especially when someone has never said they were sorry, you can stay in the Present Room even in the presence of someone who has hurt you.

Why can't people forgive? What is so hard about it? One problem is that everyone has levels of what they believe they can forgive. *I can forgive this, but I can't forgive that.* That *crosses the line.* One person's expectations may be different from someone else's. Yet unconditional forgiveness is true forgiveness—it surpasses all the preconceived levels of what we would tolerate. Anything else is still just a judgment of someone's behavior. So don't accept the ego's rationale for not forgiving someone. The more someone harms us, the greater the opportunity to express forgiveness. Unfortunately, we don't see it that way. We fail to recognize that the people who harm us most are our greatest teachers. If we can learn to forgive them, we can learn to forgive anyone, including ourselves. Ironically, when you recognize your oneness with all of life, you will no longer need to forgive because you will no longer judge anyone as guilty.

We may think it impossible to forgive all things, but we never know what we are capable of until that moment of truth arrives. One of the most telling examples of this occurred during the 2013 Blade Runner trial in South Africa. Former Olympian Oscar Pistorius was jailed for allegedly fatally shooting his girlfriend in his home. June Steenkamp, the mother of slain Reeva Steenkamp, was asked if she forgave Pistorius for killing her daughter. She answered, "It's actually important to forgive him, for me, because I don't want to live with bitterness in my life. I don't want that. I think that one has to forgive."[5] Most people would completely understand if she had said she could never forgive him, no matter what the outcome of the trial, but that's the lower self that is speaking. Obviously, June Steenkamp looked within and listened to her Higher Self. And by forgiving, she freed herself. That's not to say she'll never feel any negative emotions toward Pistorius again, but forgiveness will allow her to let them go much more quickly. She discovered the truth of how the law of forgiveness operates. It doesn't let the other person off the hook; it lets *you* off the hook.

FORGIVE AND LOVE YOURSELF

We devote great energy to beating ourselves up over things we have done or failed to do. Why do we have so much trouble forgiving ourselves? We rehash our past mistakes and behaviors, not recognizing that our regrets eat us up inside. It's always easy to look back and see how we should have done things differently, but every time you beat yourself up over something you've done in the past, you are trapped in the Past Room. You're not going to get back to the Present Room until you can forgive yourself.

The problem is, when you are stuck in regret mode, you don't understand that you need to forgive yourself to free yourself. To solve this problem, consider what's bothering you from the past. Maybe you had stopped visiting someone you now really miss because of something you heard they said, only to find out later it wasn't true. In this scenario, you would think about how you might have handled it differently and then apologize to yourself. Once you've sincerely apologized to yourself, then forgive yourself. Yes, you need to fully accept your own apology, to tell yourself, "I completely forgive you." The result is: Goodbye, regret. Hello, peace.

Just as you needed to take care of yourself before you could care for others, you need to love yourself first. The greatest love you can achieve is a love for all—but you can't get there without starting with a love for yourself.

We tend to start with loving someone else. We love them with all our heart. They are special to us. But when we do this, when we elevate someone else as being more deserving of love than others, not only do we not achieve a love for all, but we don't even manage to love ourselves. So often we hear the phrase, "True love means loving someone more than you love yourself." Although this idea makes for a great Hallmark card, it's just not true. For instance, I love my children dearly. There is no doubt in my mind that if they were crossing a street and a bus were coming at them, I would immediately jump into harm's way to push them to safety. Does that mean I love them more than I love myself? Not at all.

When you truly love yourself, you understand what it means to love *all*. When you love all people, your love for others is not limited to a "special" love you feel for certain people in your life, even your own children. When you truly love yourself, there is no decision to make about whom you'll jump in front of the bus for. You won't say, "Let me see, I'll sacrifice myself to save my wife and my children, but I'll let the bus run over my neighbor." The truly heroic are those who sacrifice themselves to save the lives of people they've never met. That was the motto of the Knights of the Roundtable. That was the behavior of the responders on 9/11. This is why we honor those in the military services. Do they sacrifice their lives to protect you because they love you more than they love themselves? No! They don't pick and choose who they are going to protect. They protect others the same as they would want to be protected themselves.

The most important relationship we have is with ourselves. More specifically, it's our relationship with our Higher Self, which is the part of us that we all share. So don't love others more than you love yourself. Love others *as* you love yourself. I want my children to know I will love them always, but this does not mean that I love only them. It means that I only love.

In the end, we all want to feel peace and love, and forgiveness brings us these feelings we crave. Still, we refuse to grant this peace to ourselves in many situations, which doesn't make sense. It's like being given a key to a door you want to go through, but instead of using the key, you keep smashing your head against the door. It just doesn't work, and you remain outside and in pain. We've been given the key to peace and serenity, but we refuse to use it. In reality, the only reason you feel others don't deserve forgiveness is that you don't feel *you* deserve it. Remember the order of priorities. Forgive yourself first, and then you will be able to forgive others. Complete forgiveness will give you the peace you crave and allow you to move back into the Present Room.

VISITING EACH ROOM

We benefit from reflecting on the past and planning for the future. One of our primary purposes on Earth is to remember the place we came from before we were born. How can we remember anything without looking back at the past? It depends. If you want to remember something you did in this lifetime, you visit the Past Room. If you want to remember who you are and where you came from, you need to be in the Present Room.

Once again, the key is awareness. If you go into the Past Room specifically to remember something that happened in your life, either good or bad, happy or sad, you need to go there intentionally. It is the *intention* that makes all the difference. While there, you must maintain awareness that you're in the Past Room. With this awareness serving as a layer of protection, you can then get what you need from the past and return to the Present Room. If you are unable to maintain this conscious divide of where you are, you can get weighed down by guilt, anger, or resentment. If you aren't aware that you're in the Past Room, these feelings feel real and present, so you don't realize you need to come back out.

If you're stuck in the Past Room and thinking about someone in the present, it doesn't mean you've moved into the Present Room. In the Present Room, not only are you focused on the now, but you're aware of your oneness with all things. If you're bringing negative feelings against another, by definition you're focused on your differences from that person and therefore can't be in the Present Room. Likewise, if you look into the past with loving thoughts, you can't be in the Past Room because you will only find fear-based thoughts there. Your thoughts are just going back in the linear concept of time to recall specific events in your life.

The Present Room focuses on the world of light. The Past and Future Rooms focus on the world of form. But regardless of where your physical form is, the room you choose to put your thoughts in becomes your perception of reality. If you believe your thoughts are in the present but they are rooted in fear, then you are not in the Present Room. If you're thinking, "I'm looking for someone to steal from right now," you're not in the Present Room. You may think you are living in the present, but your fear-based thoughts are being driven by something that happened in your past. Likewise, if your thoughts are in the past but they are rooted in love, you are still in the Present Room. Moving from room to room is not about the linear dimension of time, but about the qualitative dimension of your thoughts and the emotions they produce.

GETTING STUCK IN ONE ROOM

If you are going to get stuck in one room, for God's sake, make it the Present Room. If you get stuck in one of the fear-based rooms, you will forget the feeling of love. When you're stuck in the wrong room, you can hurt for a long time. The only way to get better is to reclaim the feeling of love.

The feeling of love is in the heart, and the heart is where your power to heal comes from. The ancient mystics understood this. Even fairytales touch on this. The Disney blockbuster *Frozen* is a perfect example.[6] At the end of the movie, the message is clear: An act of true love will thaw a frozen heart. A frozen heart has forgotten what love feels like. It's a heart suspended in the space-time continuum. It has not gone away. It has not been eliminated. It is just frozen in its present form and waiting to be thawed, waiting to remember what it truly is: love. An act of true love toward a person with a frozen heart reminds them that love heals. It reminds them that love is all there is. It allows that person to remember who they really are.

You need to ask yourself: When was the last time I performed an act of true love toward someone? When was the last time I showed true compassion to someone, even if they never showed any to me? Our ego often views others as cold, heartless people who don't deserve our love or help. In reality, they're not heartless. Their hearts may simply be frozen. Any act of kindness, compassion, or true love has the power to thaw their frozen hearts. Consequently, performing an act of true love can move you back into the Present Room. When you're stuck in the Past or Future Room, your heart is, in a sense, frozen. It is still filled with love, but you are not aware of that love. Any act of true love will reawaken your awareness of love and bring you straight into the Present Room.

It's not surprising that the award-winning song from the soundtrack to *Frozen* is titled "Let It Go." What is surprising, however, is that so many people don't get its message. The problem with most of society is that we *don't* let it go. Instead, we hold on to all the injustices we believe have been inflicted on us by the cruel people of this world. As a result, we cling to thoughts of what others have done, instead of the awareness of who we really are. This keeps us stuck in the Past Room. Until we let go of those thoughts causing negative emotions, we cannot move back to the Present Room.

THE HARDEST ROOM TO ENTER

It may seem counterintuitive, but the hardest room to enter is the Present Room. Although our Source is saying, "Come on in," we start to look within, get close, and then run back to our comfort zone. As children, we're afraid of a lot of things. One of the biggest things kids are afraid of is the dark. What kids are not afraid of is the light; as far as they're concerned, the brighter the better. How ironic that when we grow up, we're no longer afraid of the dark, but we're petrified of the light. As adults, we see the light, and we want to run screaming in the other direction. We are afraid of the light because we haven't built up trust in God. Building up that trust is not easy. Surrendering yourself to anything is scary, especially surrendering control of your life. Your ego doesn't give up easily.

After my wife Deb and I got engaged, Deb talked to a friend

who'd recently married a divorced father of two. As someone who was about to do the same, Deb sought guidance from her. So what was this friend's advice? It was to "run screaming" from me. There were way too many complications in this kind of situation, she said. She warned that Deb would have to deal with stepchildren, honor other commitments, and that we may not have enough time as a couple, among others. Fortunately for me, Deb didn't heed her advice and decided to give the man she fell in love with a chance. "Being independent of the good opinion of other people," as Abraham Maslow would put it, worked out well for both of us.[7] Too bad that when it comes to knowing God, we do often heed the advice that Deb received. Every time we get close to our Source, we get freaked out based on our past experiences and run screaming, and it takes a while to get close again. Sure enough, when that moment comes again, when we start to feel the presence of the Divine within us, we're off running.

When we finally get the courage to step into the Present Room, our eternal being is there waiting for us, inviting us in. The easiest time to access the Present Room is always in the morning. Why? Because the Present Room is simply our conscious awareness of love, and as *A Course in Miracles* teaches, all that's preventing us from experiencing that love is the barriers we put up to the awareness of love's presence. In the morning, when you first wake up, you haven't erected any barriers yet. That's why you want to follow Michael Strahan's advice from the title of his book and *Wake Up Happy*.[8] It's important to focus on these early moments because as soon as you start thinking, your thoughts—positive or negative—gain momentum. Each thought builds on the previous thought. Once you start thinking about the problems of the world, the Law of Attraction brings you more of those thoughts. On the other hand, when you wake up remembering who you are and keep focusing your thoughts on your connection to your Divine Source, *those* thoughts multiply, as does the power of your connection to all.

There is a high correlation between the room you start the day in and the room you end the day in. In other words, the longer you spend in one room in the morning, the greater the likelihood you'll spend the rest of the day there.

It's up to you which room you start your day in. If you allow your thoughts to focus immediately on your "everyday problems," you'll step right into the Past or Future Room. If, however, you focus on conscious awareness of your Higher Power, you'll enter the Present Room.

BE AWARE OF YOUR FEELINGS

To move from room to room, you have to know which room you're in at any moment. That's why the question to ask is always, "Where am I?" And while your thoughts are the key determinant of which room you are in, the answer to where you are always depends on how you feel. Your thoughts get you there, and then your feelings validate your thoughts. They are always congruent with what you are thinking. If you have fear-based thoughts, you'll have fear-based emotions. If you have loving thoughts, you will feel loving emotions. If you constantly think about whether it will rain for your son's graduation next week, you will constantly feel anxious. If you only think about the wonderful accomplishment of his college degree, you will only feel joy.

Whenever you want to know where your thoughts are, ask yourself, "How do I feel?" If you rely on your thoughts to tell you where you are, and your thoughts are controlled by the ego, you'll be fooled time and time again, because the ego is clever. It will tell you, "I'm here in the Present Room," but you'll still feel crappy. Your emotions can't lie, though. Your emotions can't say they're happy but still make you feel like crap. Unlike the ego and your thoughts, your emotions will give you an accurate reading every time.

When you go to a doctor's office, they don't ask, "How are you doing?" Instead, they ask, "How are you feeling?" The answer tells them how they can help heal you. Keep asking yourself, "How do I feel?" With all the brilliant people in the world, no one can answer this simple question for you. Ultimately, you'll get an answer from deep inside yourself because you can't get the answer from anyone or anything else. If you're honest with yourself and allow yourself to feel, that feeling will reveal where you are.

You create your experience through your thoughts, but you measure your experiences by your emotions. If you feel peace, love, and joy, you know your thoughts are in the Present Room. If you feel anger, guilt, and resentment, you know your thoughts are in the Past Room. If you feel stress, anxiety, and lack, you know your thoughts are in the Future Room. We get tripped up when we become convinced we are thinking one way but our emotions tell us something different. Our emotions are always right, because our emotions allow us to feel not only what we are thinking consciously but our subconscious thoughts, as well.

Too often we remember what someone said to hurt our feelings, but we forget their little act of kindness that made us feel good. Those are the feelings we need to remember. Remember the feeling when you were a child and learned to ride a bike for the first time. Remember the feeling when you were a teen and had your first kiss. Remember the feeling when you were an adult and first got engaged. Remember that feeling. Remember the feeling of all the people and experiences you loved. Soak them up in the moment. Take all those feelings and combine them into one complex and wonderful feeling. Now remember: *That* is who you are. Why do we let others lead us to believe we are less than that?

HWJF: HOW WOULD JESUS FEEL?

We have all heard the expression "What Would Jesus Do?" There is even a shortened version, WWJD. The concept of trying to emulate the Prince of Peace is commendable, but it is flawed if we're trying to figure out what Christ would do while still clinging to our belief in separation. We may believe Jesus would forgive in any given situation, but if we layer our own thoughts and judgments on top of our idea of him, we'll come up with reasons why we can't do the same thing.

A better question to ask ourselves is, "How Would Jesus Feel?" or HWJF. Only if we're coming from the same perception as Christ can we know what Jesus would do and, therefore, *do* what Jesus would do. If we feel only love, as Jesus would, we can express only love in any situation. We can forgive in any situation. Then, and only then, will we be doing what Jesus would do. So if we can answer the question HWJF, we'll discover the answer to WWJD.

It all comes back to knowledge and perception. We can't look at the world through the eyes of separation and expect to do what the masters did. The only way to do as Jesus would is to see the world through the eyes of Christ, which comes from the place of oneness. True knowledge is the realization that only love is real. Jesus had this knowledge. It is that knowledge of the true world, and not the perception we create, that allows us to do as Jesus would. To obtain that knowledge, we need to feel what Christ felt, which is love and compassion. When we feel love and compassion, we have just moved back into the Present Room.

TRUSTING YOUR INTUITION

I'd been single for many years before I was introduced to my wife, and we first spoke over the phone. For some reason, even though I wouldn't characterize those initial phone conversations as having gone very well, I told my friend Larry I was going to marry Deb before I ever met her in person. I'd certainly never made such a prediction before, but there was some combination of feelings and a knowing that led me to that conclusion. Call it intuition.

When we trust in our Higher Power and feel it in our heart, it can lead to remarkable discoveries. But too many of us don't. We let the ego trick us into believing something, even though we don't feel it to be true. This can get us into big trouble. But when we recognize a "knowing" in our heart, it can lead to the most incredible feeling: unconditional love. This is the feeling we get when we connect with that eternal being we all share inside. It's also the feeling we get when we feel our connection to another human being without expecting anything in return.

FOCUS ON THE SPACE

The Past Room is filled with all your thoughts about who you think you are, based on what you've done and what others have done to you. The Future Room is filled with all your thoughts about what might prevent you from achieving your goals in life. It can also be filled with thoughts about controlling other people's actions so they don't interfere with the image you've created of yourself. The Present Room is initially filled with *no thoughts*. It is the awareness of the space between your thoughts.

That doesn't mean you never have any thoughts in the Present Room. It just means you don't become attached to the thoughts in the Present Room. As negative thoughts come in, you acknowledge them and let them go. When you hear hurtful words from other people, you acknowledge them and let them go. As you witness disturbing events, you acknowledge them and let them go. Your awareness never changes, and you continuously remain centered in the space between the thoughts, the words, and the objects that used to drag you down. Focusing on the space between you and negativity keeps you in the Present Room.

You feel so drained in the Past and Future Rooms because you're using up so much energy processing thoughts that contradict with the thoughts of your Higher Self. When you are in the Present Room, you are not influenced by negative thoughts about what people think about you or what they've done to you. Instead, you become the receiver of the thoughts that your eternal being thinks about you and others. So when you observe people from the Present Room, you can feel compassion and love for them because you see them for who they really are—an eternal being in a physical body. In the Present Room, you can't help but feel happy because there is nothing to prevent it—no worries about what you will do tomorrow, no anger over what someone said to you yesterday—just joy. Just love. Just bliss. That is how we are supposed to feel.

Think about it. When we first come into this world, we all start in the Present Room. Therefore, the most important principle of moving from room to room is to avoid being pulled out of the Present Room in the first place. How do we get pulled out? By what we think, what we hear, what we see.

What we think: The biggest culprits pulling us out of the Present Room are our thoughts, because we seldom monitor them. If we're unaware of what we're thinking throughout the day, we can't recognize the impact our thoughts have on our emotions. By focusing on the space between thoughts, we are no longer bound to the negative emotions these thoughts may produce.

What we hear: Even if we monitor our thoughts closely and try to think happy thoughts, we constantly hear what other people say. As we hear these words, they can trigger memories and release a flood of negative emotions. The ensuing action is swift— we're yanked from the happy thoughts of the Present Room and thrust into the emotional turmoil of the Past Room. Words only have power over us to the degree that we allow them. By focusing on the space between the words, and not giving validity to those words, we are no longer bound to the negative emotions they may produce.

What we see: The most frequent factors pulling us out of the Present Room are the objects and people we see every day. Wherever we go, regardless of what we think or hear, we're constantly looking at people, objects, and unfolding action. When we witness something, the ego is ready to pounce on it and make assumptions or simply pass judgment based on our perceived differences. As soon as we start judging instead of observing, we've been pulled out of the Present Room. If instead we focus on the space between objects, we are no longer bound to the negative emotions they may produce, because we no longer perceive ourselves as separate from what we see.

In the end, if we focus on the space between, we're not focusing on what we're thinking, hearing, or seeing but on the feeling of alignment with our eternal being. When we feel no negative emotions from what we think, hear, or see, we are left with nothing but positive emotions. That's when we know we have moved between rooms and found our way back to the Present Room.

CHAPTER 6

THE MOVIE THEATER

We simply watch this karmic movie with a secret delight, like
watching the wiggles of our own fingers, which see themselves as
"others." With great love and humor, we sport in the playground of
this external universe. With a secret smile, we know that all others
are our own self externalized. Then we play this game with great
joy. This is true freedom, and the only spirituality there is.

—YOGA PROVERB

YOGA PHILOSOPHY TEACHES THAT THE WORLD IS LIKE A MOVIE
in which we have a starring role. Many people can relate to this
concept, but what they seldom grasp is that while we are the stars
of the production, we are not the director. When we realize our
Higher Power is the real director, we can take our cues from that
power in every moment of our lives. This understanding frees us
from having to figure out where to go, what to do, and what to say.

Most miraculous is that once we accept that we are not directing this movie of our lives, we can enjoy watching it unfold with our thoughts in the Present Room.

VIEW YOUR LIFE AS A MOVIE

It makes little difference whether you view your life as a play or a movie. What matters is your ability to participate in your life movie while taking guidance from your higher power. To do that, you have to separate your awareness from your thoughts, because some part of "you" needs to be aware you are in a movie while the other part of "you" remains in the movie.

There are few better examples of viewing life in this observer and participant way than in the movie *The Matrix*.[1] Keanu Reeves' character, Neo, finds out life as he knows it is not real. Instead, he learns that his existence in the titular matrix is a façade. Knowing this grants him the ability to manipulate the matrix while being aware that he is truly living outside of it. What if you learned something similar about your life and that you have access to powers you were not aware of? Maybe not scaling buildings in a single bound—but what if you could attract people and circumstances into your life by knowing they were going to appear? The mystics tell us this power to attract things into our lives is possible.

From a Three Rooms perspective, the way you feel determines the room your thoughts are in, and the movie of your life is a physical manifestation of the way you feel. So whichever room your thoughts are in determines the movie you are watching in that moment because how you feel is the main determinant of what you attract into your life. If your thoughts are stuck in the Past Room, then the Past Movie will reflect your experience of life from that perspective. If you are constantly worried about the future, those fear-based thoughts will be reflected in the Future Movie. Finally, if you are aligned with your eternal being in the Present Room, the positive emotions you experience will be projected outward as the Present Movie. Let's watch how the movie of your life can change based on which room your thoughts are in. Imagine you walk into a movie theater where three movies are playing, and they are all about your life. You get to choose which movie you want to watch. One door is labeled "The Past Theater," one door is labeled "The Future Theater," and one door is labeled "The Present Theater."

THE PAST MOVIE

The Past Movie depicts our experience of life today based on mental projections we have created from past experiences. These stored up images of unpleasant experiences can feel as if they are repeating in our lives, and whenever daily events remind us of anything we are trying to avoid thinking about, they take us back to the Past Room and can trigger feelings of anger, bitterness, and resentment. Because of these dramatic stakes, the Past Movie would be classified in film genre as a drama.

You look at the three doors, and you choose the door that says "The Past Theater." When you sit down inside, you see yourself as you are today, living in today's world without having let go of the past. You can hear the thoughts the character on screen is thinking—and that character is you. As you watch the movie, you see yourself in your car on your way to a job interview. All you are thinking about is how little sleep you had the night before and how tired you are. The you on screen feels wiped out and hopes some coffee will give you a jolt. You spot a Starbucks at the last minute and cut off two cars as you pull into the parking lot.

As you enter the store, your agitated mind continues to wander. You pay for your coffee, but people are in front of you. *Why did I watch that last show last night? I'm so wiped out, and I have to do this interview now.*

Whoa! You bump right into the person in front of you and splash coffee all over your shirt.

"Are you kidding me!" you scream at the man.

He shoots back a nasty glare and fires off, "What the heck are you talking about? You just rammed right into me."

After several more unpleasantries, you watch yourself walk out of the store, your shirt soaked in coffee and your mind racing. You decide to go home and change. On your way back, both your car and your mind are speeding. *I didn't even notice that jerk in front of me. I can't believe it. Now I'm going to be late.* As you rush to the interview, you notice a car stopped on the side of the road with the hood up. Some poor guy's car broke down. *Wait, was that Tim? Too late. I don't have time to help, anyway.*

Once you finally arrive for your interview, you find out there's going to be an extra fifteen-minute wait. You feel frustrated and unhappy. If you'd known they were running late, you wouldn't have raced there so fast. Maybe this is because the office is very disorganized. *Why do I want to work for someone so disorganized?*

During the interview, your mind keeps returning to your bad experience in the coffee shop. You feel resentful, flustered, and you have trouble focusing on the questions you're being asked. When it's over, you're glad to get out of there. You're told they will call to let you know if you got the job. You still can't believe they asked many of the questions they asked. It should have been a breeze, but you didn't answer the way you wanted.

On the way home, you can't stop thinking what a disaster the interview was. *That guy was a real jerk for asking those questions. If he has a big say in the matter, then I am not getting this job, I just know it. It's all because of him!*

That night during dinner, you tell your wife this interview didn't really matter because the office seemed very disorganized. First, they made you wait, and then they asked a lot of the same questions as the previous interview. When your wife points out that fifteen minutes is a common wait time, you get defensive.

When the phone rings, the words on the other end are clear. "We are sorry . . ." When you hang up, you tell your wife, "I knew it. It's a good thing I didn't get the job. I didn't want to work for them, anyway." You feel satisfied—but not for long. You watch yourself go to bed brooding about what you said during the interview. *I should have prepared more.*

The "you" watching the movie has had enough. You can feel the guilt that your character is projecting on the screen.

When you think of viewing your life like this, you can see how the Past Room's influence created an unwanted situation for you in this movie. Your first reaction may be *Who was that? I don't act that way. But it seemed so real.*

THE FUTURE MOVIE

You find yourself staring at the next door, which says "The Future Movie." This brings a bit of relief because you're very interested in your future. Doesn't everybody wish they could see their future? You understand there are risks, but that doesn't stop you. You turn the handle and step into the theater.

The Future Movie shows our present lives as mental projections of who we think we are and where we think we are going. The mere thought of these projections potentially being challenged brings stress and anxiety. In the Future Movie, we are not using our imagination to help create the future we desire. Instead, we are focusing on all the things that could happen to us in the present that can prevent the future we desire. Not surprisingly, this movie is also a drama.

When you step into the Future Theater, you take your seat and immediately realize what you're watching on the screen is not set in the future. You're in the same place in this movie as in the Past Movie—in your car, driving to a job interview. But this time, you are much more anxious. You see the stress on your face and feel the tension. As you drive, you can hear your mind wondering what will happen if you don't get the job. *If I don't get something else soon, how will I make my rent payments?* You hear your mind racing on-screen and watch yourself pull into Starbucks.

You enter Starbucks and see the line. You're worried about not having enough time to get to the interview. *But I really want my caffeine, so I'll give it a try. If the people in front of me place big orders, I definitely won't have enough time. I can't believe how insensitive people are.*

You finally order your coffee and then wait in another line for cream and sugar. *This guy in front of me is so slow. Hurry up*, you keep saying to yourself. Just as before, he turns around and the two of you collide, spilling your coffee all over your shirt.

"Damn! What the heck are you doing?" you scream.

"Me?" is his response. "You just rammed right into me!"

After a few more unpleasantries, your mind races ahead to your interview. You need to go home and change your shirt and tie, but you're panicking that you'll never make it on time. You rush home anyway, your mind obsessing about missing the interview. You pass a car broken down on the side of the road and notice it's your friend Tim. *Sorry, Tim*, you think as you drive right past him. *I won't make the job interview if I stop for you.*

When you finally arrive at the office for the interview, you have to wait fifteen minutes. Your mind races ahead. *Maybe they already hired someone. I probably don't have a chance for this job. What am I going to do now?* These thoughts continue right through the interview. *I don't know why I'm answering these questions. They've already hired someone else.* Afterward, you're told they will call you tonight to let you know if you got the job.

Once you're home, you realize they didn't say what time they'd call. *What if they don't call? If they don't call me by ten o'clock, maybe I should call them. If I don't get this job, I'm in deep trouble. What am I going to do? This stinks. I better start working on a back-up plan.*

That night at dinner you tell your wife you think they've already hired someone else. You need to start looking at other companies, maybe even other industries. "Let's wait and see what they say first," she says reassuringly. But you know what they're going to say. The phone rings and the words on the other end are clear. "We are sorry . . ."

"I told you," you say to your wife. "I have to do something else for work, but I don't know what."

"Slow down!" she exclaims. "Let's take this one day at a time."

But the "you" on the screen doesn't want to hear it.

The "you" in the movie seat has heard enough too.

Outside, you shake your head, trying to figure out what's going on. When you think of viewing your life like this, you can see how the Future Room's influence created more unwanted outcomes in this movie. The two movies were so similar, yet you felt so different. They both seemed like a bad dream.

THE PRESENT MOVIE

When we watch the movie of our life through the eyes of love, compassion, and non-judgment, what we see on the screen completely changes. We spend so much time looking at the world through the eyes of the ego and trying to deal with all the problems we have created with our own guilt and judgment, but these are just perceived problems we created ourselves. Instead of asking our Higher Power to resolve these perceived problems, we should team up with our Higher Power and watch the Present Movie. We'll find that those problems are not even in the script. Instead of conflict, we'll experience wholeness, peace, and joy. That is what love feels like. This movie is better characterized as a romantic comedy.

Why a comedy? Because we need to be able to poke fun at ourselves. If you take yourself too seriously, rest assured that others will find humor at your expense. That's why it's so important to try to find humor in life every day. As Charlie Chaplin said, "A day without laughter is a day wasted."

As you sit down in the Present Theater, you see a now-familiar scene. Once again, you are in your car driving to a job interview. But this time, you're playing relaxing music and picturing what it will be like to work for this company.

You decide to get some coffee, so you pull into a Starbucks. You pay for your coffee and wait in another line for cream and sugar. The person in front of you seems to be in a big hurry. You stand back a bit, giving him some room, but after he gets his cream, he turns around sharply in your direction. You move out of his way and bump into the person behind you. You apologize to them, but you can feel the hot coffee spilled on to the back of your shirt. You shake your head as you realize you have to go home and change your shirt. But it's okay. You should still to be able to make the interview on time.

After you stop home and change your shirt, you're driving toward the interview when you see a car stuck on the side of the road. As you slow down, you notice it's your friend Tim. You hesitate for a second, realizing you may be late for your interview, but decide to pull over anyway and ask if he needs help.

"You are a life saver," he says. "My car overheated, and I left my cell phone at home."

You give him your phone, and he calls for a tow truck. When he hands it back, he asks where you're headed.

"I'm actually going to a job interview right now. I think it's time for a change in my career."

"I can't believe you just said that," Tim replies. "I thought about calling you last week. Our company is opening up a new division right here in town, and your skill set would be ideal to run it. But I didn't think you would ever leave your company."

"That's very interesting," you say. "That's exactly the type of opportunity I was hoping for. I'll tell you what, I'm committed to this job interview today, but I'll call you tomorrow."

"Great," says Tim. "I look forward to speaking with you."

You're late arriving at the office, but you're prepared to accept any negative consequences. Instead, you learn that the interview was delayed by fifteen minutes, so you're actually on time. During the interview, you focus on the questions and answer them as honestly and thoughtfully as you can. Before you know it, the interview is over and you're heading home. You're not sure whether you are supposed to get this job or if you should take the job Tim mentioned. Rather than dwell on this dilemma, you turn it over to your Higher Power, willing to accept whichever option turns out to be the best opportunity for you. You think about your win-win scenario and smile.

That night over dinner, you tell your wife about your chance encounter with Tim. You also say you thought the interview went well. You answered all the questions as well as you could have. It will all turn out exactly as it should, you assure her.

Later that evening, the phone rings. You listen to the words on the other end of the line. "We are sorry . . ." You smile as you turn to your wife. "Well, it looks like I'm supposed to work with Tim," you say.

WHO'S YOUR DIRECTOR?

After you leave the theaters, you stand outside trying to make sense of what just happened. All three movies seemed so real, yet they were all so different. The first two had so much more chatter. An endless stream of thoughts distracted the main character. How can anyone function like that? But it wasn't anyone—it was you. Then you realize that you do this all the time.

During the Present Movie, there were no distractions. Your character could be witness to everything going on around you. There was no worrying about the outcome. In the Present Movie, you simply allowed everything to unfold with no resistance, yet you were still productive. You were *in* the world but not *of* the world.

The room you are currently in is your perceived reality, so wherever your thoughts are at any moment dictates your experience of life. Likewise, the room you are in determines which movie you are watching, because the perception that you project on to the screen determines your reality.

The movie of your life is always changing, but the one element not changing is the viewer of the movie and its main character—you. But if your thoughts are in the Past Room, you will be filled with fear, anger, and regrets, feelings that are reflected in the movie of your life. If your thoughts are in the Future Room, you will worry about what might happen, rather than experiencing what is happening. Only when your thoughts are in the Present Room are you fully aware of living in the present moment. Same main character. Same life. Different life experiences.

After watching the three different movies, it certainly doesn't seem like they share the same director. They don't. In short, the Past and Future Movies are the ego's interpretation of the world we see, while the Present Movie is your Higher Power's interpretation.

The ego directs the Past and Future Movies. It has to work twice as hard to keep you engaged. It fills your mind with endless chatter and fearful thoughts. Conversely, your Higher Self directs the Present Movie—even when it feels like it is simply sitting back and watching the Present Movie with you. It is there for guidance and comfort at all times—but you don't just listen to it; you *feel* it.

The ego loves dramas. Not only does it want to direct the Past and Future Movies, but it wants you to be engrossed in those movies. The ego is constantly trying to pull you out of the Present Room because it wants to absorb you into the Past and Future Movies. At that point, the ego is running the show. In fact, the ego, or your lower self, doesn't even want you to know there is a movie going on.

On the other hand, the Holy Spirit, or your Higher Self, wants to watch the movie with you. It wants you to see all the beauty in your life through your Present Movie, and it wants you to recognize all the silliness going on in other people's lives as well.

When you watch the Present Movie, you can immediately recognize which theater everyone else is in. When the ego directs them to act selfishly, you know exactly where such behavior comes from. You don't blame them, because you are aware they are Divine beings just like you; they are just sitting in the wrong theater, watching the wrong movie.

CHANGE YOUR SEAT

There is only one constant in all three movies: the *you* sitting in the theater watching the movies. That is your Higher Self. The real you sits in the seat watching, and the real you never changes. So, be the audience. Be the one sitting in the theater seat and not the one up on the screen.

What you project on the screen is what you will see. Which movie do you want to watch? Remember, it's just a projection. In the Present Movie, your Higher Self is projecting on to the screen. In the other movies, your lower (or false) self is projecting on to the screen. *A Course in Miracles* says miracles are simply a shift in perception. To shift your perception, change seats from one theater to another; you will change the projection. Then your experience of life will change, in one holy instant.

Every moment of your life runs simultaneously in each of the three theaters, and what you experience in life is directly related to the theater you choose to watch it in. By watching any of the movies, you are unknowingly separating your awareness from your thoughts. Once you do that, you are empowered to move from one movie theater to another. So ask yourself, "How does the movie of my life make me feel?" If you identify with the person in the movie, the ego is in charge and you feel separate from everyone else.

If you identify with the person *watching* the movie, your Higher Self is in charge and you feel oneness with everyone else. Can you imagine if everyone in the world sat in the Present Theater for one moment? Their lives would change instantly. The world would change instantly as well. If you want to change your life, then change your seat. If you change your seat, you will change the world

Michael Singer, in his enlightening book *The Untethered Soul*, describes a seat of awareness in which you start to experience the spiritual energy called Shakti.[2] In the Hindu faith, Shakti is a divine cosmic energy that moves through the entire universe. When you sit in this seat of awareness, Singer explains, you can feel the Shakti flowing through you. That is what happens when you watch the movie of your life from the Present Theater. But if your thoughts are in the Past Room and you are consumed with your melodrama, you don't realize you are caught up in the day-to-day trivia of the world. The Past Theater shows the movie of your life from this perspective. When you become aware of this, you can move instantly into the Present Theater and watch the movie of your life as if it were a comedy; when you are in your right mind, it can be quite humorous to watch other people who are not in theirs.

IMPROVE YOUR VISION

There are billions of people in the world who wear prescription eyeglasses. These glasses give them the ability to see things that they otherwise couldn't. The change in perception that these glasses give their wearers allows them to interact with the world in safer and more informed ways. Similarly, we all have the opportunity to see the world better by changing our perception with a simple tool: the perspective of your Higher Self, the director of your Present Movie. When you do this, you don't need to make anything happen. You don't even need to put a pair of lenses over your own eyes. Instead, you are able to fully see the unfolding of your life according to the director's plan.

When you watch your life unfold in the Present Theater, you see with the vision of the mystics. Wayne Teasdale, who devoted his life to spirituality and service, tells us in his book *The Mystic Heart*, "Mystical seeing, which also depends on self-knowledge, is really the gift of perspective, of being able to see everything in its proper place."[3] Mystical seeing, therefore, is seeing everything from the proper perspective, or from the right theater. All the mystics see from this perspective.

If you could see through the eyes of our creator, see things around you that you would not be able to otherwise, wouldn't you want to experience that? Well, maybe you can. It all starts with understanding how our physical sight works. When light enters our eye, it must pass through the cornea before it reaches the pupil. The light then passes through the pupil to the lens of the eye, which adjusts the path of the light and brings it into focus on to the retina, the receiving area at the back of our eye. If the cornea is scratched or damaged, however, it alters the light that reaches the pupil.

Now, instead of looking at how physical light travels through the cornea and the pupil, let's use a metaphor about the teacher and the pupil. The teacher (our creator) wants to send light (knowledge, love) to the pupil (the creation, or us). However, the light (understanding) must first go through the cornea (our thoughts), which are in the way of the pupil (you). To receive the light from the teacher, the pupil must remove the thoughts blocking the path. A healthy cornea (positive thoughts) will allow the light right through to the pupil. A scratched or damaged cornea (negative thoughts) will block the light from reaching the pupil.

If the pupil receives the light, its purpose is not to keep it for itself but to pass it through to the lens (our Higher Self). The lens can then adjust the path of light and bring the world into focus for you. With this new projection, you are viewing the world directly through the eyes of the creator. That vision is the Present Movie of your life.

WATCHING A DRAMA VS. LIVING A DRAMA

If we go to the movies and watch a drama, we enjoy all the heartache and sadness on the big screen because we know it is disconnected from our actual lives. After all, we are just sitting in a movie theater. But in our real lives, when far less severe things happen, we get distraught.

For example, The Godfather movies were some of the top-grossing movies of all time. They portrayed all kinds of extreme behaviors—murder, deceit, revenge—but when people walked out of the theater, they'd say, "Wow, what an incredible movie!" Then, on their way home, if someone canceled dinner plans with them, they may think it was the end of the world. "How could they do this to me? I was so looking forward to it. I am never making plans with them again!"

Do you see what's happening? The difference is that when we watch a movie, we have a willing suspension of disbelief. We accept that it is not real. Well, in real life we need a willing suspension of *false belief*—a suspension of believing in all the untrue things we have been taught, such as resentment, greed, and revenge. We have the ability to achieve this suspension of false belief by stepping into the Present Theater and watching our life movies with the same humor and appreciation we watch all other movies and plays with.

If you really understood that your life was just a movie, you would be better able to handle all the stressful challenges in your life. Of course, we all face different degrees of challenges. Still, we watch a movie and we don't hold the actors accountable for what they do because we know they're just acting. But in the movie of our life, we hold everyone accountable for what they do. Why is that different? What if we took the behavior we see in the movies as literally as we do in our everyday lives? Can you imagine Leonardo DiCaprio walking down the street, seeing Jack Nicholson approaching, then walking right up and punching him in the face because he smashed his hand in *The Departed*? Of course not, that's ridiculous. Nicholson was just acting. Well, guess what? You, and everybody around you, are just actors in a movie—the movie of your lives. When you grasp that, you grasp everything.

WHAT IS REAL?

Just for a moment, picture what it will be like when you die. When you pass away, "here" will be your present consciousness, and "there" will be the memory of the time you spent on Earth. Only one of these "places" can be real. If the time you spent on Earth was real, what do you call the present consciousness you experience in the afterlife, or Heaven? And if that consciousness that you experience in Heaven is real, what do you call the time spent in your body on Earth?

The only thing real is the eternal, Divine consciousness you came from and will return to. That is the consciousness we all transition to after our physical lives are over. That Divine consciousness, Heaven on Earth, is the same consciousness you want to tap into while in your physical body. It can only be experienced in the Present Room.

So instead of waiting until your physical body expires to look back on the movie of your life, watch it while you're still in it. What's the difference? If you watch it while you are still acting in it, you get to enjoy it a lot more. Picture yourself in Heaven, looking back on the movie of your life. Do you think you will feel stressed out watching it in Heaven? Do you think you'll worry about what other people say? No? So watch the movie of your life right now, and don't worry. Just think about how you'd like your life to go from this point forward. Imagine the type of life you would like to live and the type of person you would like to be. Then watch your life unfold from where you are right now to where you want to be. Watch that movie with the same focus that you use to binge on Netflix shows. Go to that place—that which is real, eternal, changeless—and then you will really delight in the humor of this thing we call life.

PLAYING DIFFERENT CHARACTERS

You may be the main character in the movie of your life, but you are also *all* the characters. Think about it. If we all share the same

Divine consciousness on the inside, then everyone you see is an extension of you.

Yes, you are the man with the hard hat at the construction site you're passing. You are the taxi driver who doesn't seem to know where he's going. You are the man on the corner asking for some change. It's not hard to imagine; the talented actor and comedian Eddie Murphy has played multiple roles in six different movies. If you want to smile, watch the movie of your life with the premise that you are playing all the different roles. When you look around and see other people, you will be a bit kinder and more helpful to them if you know their eternal being is connected to yours.

Some of the things we like so much about watching a movie are the surprises. People who appear early on in what seem like insignificant roles turn up later and become very significant characters. Your physical life is no different. If someone keeps popping up out of the blue, it's time to ask yourself why they keep appearing. Maybe next time that person shows up (because you know they will) you might not want to turn away but rather say, "Hi, what's up with you?" Maybe they have information you're supposed to know.

Theodor Geisel, a.k.a. Dr. Seuss, had his first manuscript rejected twenty-seven times. He was ready to give up his dream of being a published author when he bumped into a friend who had just become an editor in the children's division of a publishing house. Seuss later said that if he'd been walking on the other side of the street, he probably would have never been published. But what if he'd seen his friend and just hadn't felt like talking to him, so he'd ducked into a store and let him walk by? Then, too, he would never have become an author who inspired children throughout the world.

Life presents us with opportunities left and right, but we're just not ready to accept them. We tend to avoid certain people when we don't think they can help us, even though we can't possibly know that. Other times we think we're just too damn busy to take a minute to talk to someone. But we are only able to take the opportunities that life gives us if we are open to them. Learning to view other people as expressions of Divine consciousness helps us to perceive the potential that they have to meaningfully impact our lives (and for us to do the same for them).

MOVIE RERUNS

We've all watched a favorite television show or movie multiple times. With comedies, it doesn't matter if we have watched the same scene ten times; we still laugh at all the same moments. With tragedies, we get our tissues and prepare for a good cry. With action movies, we grab our popcorn and brace ourselves for the same adventure. We seem to enjoy watching the same stories over and over again. In real life, we're no different.

The movie of our life repeats itself like a rerun. If something doesn't work out the way we hoped, we keep going back to the past to focus on what we did wrong, and that's the frequency we stay tuned in to. Consequently, the Law of Attraction ensures that the movie keeps following the same plotline. You may wish to change the circumstances of your life, but if you keep watching the Past Movie, all you'll ever see are reruns. Only in the Present

Theater will you see original movies, with scenes you previously imagined to be true for yourself.

TRANSFORM BY WATCHING THE PRESENT MOVIE

In every moment, we can choose which movie we want to watch. You can't sit in the Future Theater with fear-based thoughts projected on to the screen and expect the same results as in the Present Theater. It will never happen.

By concentrating too much on what is outside of us, we move from *watching* the movie of our life to being *in* the movie. Once in the movie, you lose awareness that there is a movie. Once you lose that awareness, you get stuck in the movie. You have now moved from the Present Theater to the Past or Future Theater.

The only way to return to watching the Present Movie is to become aware that you're in a different theater. To change theaters, you need to be conscious that you are focusing on fear-based thoughts. In any moment, you need to know what you're thinking and ask yourself the question, "Where am I?" To answer that, you must be aware of how you feel, which will tell you which movie you are watching. Then, and only then, can you begin watching the Present Movie again. In other words, you can identify with the person in the movie, or you can identify with the person watching the movie. Either way, that's your identity.

If you start watching the Present Movie, your life begins a transformation. As you observe everything you say and do with love and compassion, the world around you instantly transforms.

The screenplay is rewritten. That's because the life you experience is based on the thoughts you have about who you believe you are and the feelings you have in your heart. If you are aligned with your inner being and filled with feelings of love, your experience in the physical world will reflect that consciousness.

CHAPTER 7

I Am Who?

I AM my I AM presence, and I AM one with
the I AM presence of all humanity.[1]
–PATRICIA COTA ROBLES

I AM. THERE ARE NO TWO MORE IMPORTANT WORDS IN THE English language. Many have written about these words but few better than minister and mystic Emmet Fox. Describing the phrase *I am*, he says, "Only you can say I Am. That is your real identity, the presence of God in you, the Indwelling Christ."[2]

THE POWER OF *I AM*

Whatever you put after *I am* is what you will experience. If you say, "I am a crappy student," "I am a terrible dancer," or "I am a poor listener," then you will be those things. But if you say, "I am a diligent student," "I am a beautiful dancer," or "I am an attentive listener," then that is what you will experience. Only you can define yourself.

Too often we choose weakness when we describe ourselves. Even when people say, "I am what I am," they usually mean it in a derogatory manner. "I know I'm a terrible cook. What can I say? I am what I am." Little do people realize how right they are when they say these things. Saying, "I am what I am" is the same as saying, "I am what I choose to believe I am."

But there's another way of thinking about this phrase. The second *I am* in "I am what I am" is really about what you define yourself as, and the first *I am* is simply validating who you are. Whether you say, "I am what I am" or "I am what I choose to believe I am," you cannot prevent your declaration from coming true. It is a self-fulfilling prophecy.

We are all defined by our concept of who we are, and our lives are a direct reflection of that concept, whether we are cognizant of it or not. We use the words "I am" all the time without realizing their transformative power. So next time you hear yourself say, "I am—," think about how you just defined yourself and then watch how those words manifest in your physical reality.

REMOVE THE "NOT"

Many of us are very good at adding the "not" to the "I am." *I am not good enough. I am not fast enough. I am not smart enough. I am not pretty enough.* If you want to change your experience of who you are, remove the "not." Instead, declare to yourself, "I am." The only word that should ever follow "I am not" is "alone." *I am not alone.* Say it. Know it. It will bring you comfort. It is the realization that not only are you connected to your *I am* presence, but you are also connected to everyone else's.

Ironically, most of us have it backwards. We want a certain experience in life, but our concept of ourselves doesn't fit with the experience we desire, so we make what we desire impossible. If you believe you lack in your life and that you are "not" something, then you can never "be" that something. Start with what you want to be and declare that to be true, instead of declaring, "I am not . . ." while hoping it's not true.

Yes, these are only words, but they can negate our power. It's one thing to talk about the kind of person we want to be. It's another to state the kind of person we are not. When we spend too much time talking about what we want, we don't allow ourselves to feel the guidance from within, the force that manifests it. When you use words, you need to understand there is just as much power in *I am not* as there is in *I am.* They both start with "I am." Whatever follows those words will be true for you.

Your *I am* presence is simply the presence of God individualized in each of us. There is only one light, and we all share it. The light is Divine consciousness, which we all have access to. I do. You do. We all do. In that consciousness, which you can only be aware of in the Present Room, there is no concept of "I am not." So next time someone tries to tell you, "You are not," I hope you have a good laugh because that means you're not in the wrong room—they are.

I AM VS. *I WANT*

How many times have you heard someone say, "I want to be a better person" or "I will be a good person"? People think that saying, "I will be" is a lot better than saying, "I want to be" because it's more affirmative. But it's really the same thing, because you are still saying, "I am not this thing right now." In truth, "I want to be" and "I will be" are only acknowledgments that you are not those things right now. "I want to be a better person" is the same as saying, "I am not a good enough person." If you want to be a good person, cut right to the chase and say, "I am a good person."

We tend to think "I want to be" and "I will be" are positive affirmations that will get us to where we want to go. But these affirmations don't work that way. They don't reveal the path to our goals. We still need to figure that out on our own. Even when we go out and "just do it," we don't always know if what we're doing will get us where we want to be. People become frustrated all the time by busting their butts, "doing" all the right things, and still not achieving what they hoped for. This is not from lack of trying or doing but because they can't possibly know what to do in all situations to get to that desired end state.

Only an *I am* statement can lead us down the true path to achieving what we desire. The *I am* declaration also gets us where we'd like to be with the least amount of resistance. When we imagine the place we want to be in life and take ownership of it by declaring, "I am it," we can participate in the Present Movie of our life according to the direction of our Higher Self.

We will never be good at something until we say, "I am good at this now" and allow ourselves to become it. You will never be a good person or a better bowler until you visualize yourself as having those qualities right now. When you start from the place where you already are a good bowler instead of the place where you "want to be a good bowler" or even you "will be a good bowler," you will find yourself putting in the effort and practice that all good bowlers put in, and your bowling score will improve because you've made the shift to the perspective of someone who is already skilled.

Too often, people dream about where they want to be in their lives and wonder why they never get there. They spend their time thinking about what they want to be or acquire instead of who they are and what they have. *I want to be famous. I want to be rich. I want a new car. I want a great job.* By focusing on "I want" instead of "I am," you don't change who you are in the present, so you're unlikely to change your current situation in any way that will help you attain these desires. When you shift to "I am," you start to become the person capable of achieving all the things you desire. *I am a hard worker. I am a loyal friend. I am a creative person.* When you focus on the *I am*s instead of the *I want*s, you attract all those things into your life.

This is especially true if you modify your "I want" to something that will more tangibly reflect the effect the want would have on your life. Instead of saying, "I want to be rich," you can say, "I am capable of supporting myself and my family," and you'll find that the right opportunities come your way to take care of your financial situation. You may not make a million dollars, but you will see the benefit of attaining your desire fulfilled and appreciate it. While the Law of Attraction manifests our reality, the Law of Assumption is the creative force behind it. We have a hard time grasping the fact that we are what we imagine ourselves to be because we keep making the same mistakes over and over, which subconsciously creates that which we wish to avoid instead of consciously creating what we wish to experience.

In 1952, Neville Goddard wrote *The Power of Awareness*, in which he describes the creative power of the Law of Assumption in this way: "By desiring to be other than what you are, you can create an ideal of the person you want to be and assume that you are already that person. If this assumption is persisted in until it becomes your dominant feeling, the attainment of your ideal is inevitable."[3]

The movie *A Knight's Tale* offers a perfect example of someone imagining who he would like to be, envisioning it as if he'd already become it, and taking ownership by declaring it in an *I am* statement.[4] Heath Ledger plays the role of William, a poor thatcher in medieval times. His father wants a better life for him and tells William he can "change his stars"—in other words, he can be whatever he wants to be. Over time, William imagines himself as a knight, and future events unfold to give him the opportunity to become a knight under a fictitious noble name. He assumes not only the role of a knight, jousting in tournaments, but also the spirit of a knight, conducting himself with integrity and honor.

Later in the movie, William is exposed as an impostor because he wasn't born into this status. He is about to be thrown into the stockade when his friends tell him to run to save his life. But he refuses. He doesn't say, "I am not running because this isn't fair" or "I am not running because I should be able to be a knight." Instead, he says, "I cannot run. *I am* a knight." Because he already made that statement and changed his consciousness to be in line with what he desired to be, a series of events unfolded to bring about what he already assumed to be true. Eventually, he is dubbed a true knight, assuming the identity he had already become in his imagination. His experience in his physical life caught up with his experience in his consciousness.

When you change your consciousness, what you have become will come to fruition in your physical world. When you change your consciousness, you can change your stars.

MIXING YOUR *I AM* STATEMENT WITH LOVE

By now, you should understand that your thoughts are important, but thoughts alone don't always create the world you want to experience. When your thoughts are coupled with love or fear, they produce the feelings you project into the world. These feelings are the real creative force in your life.

If you mix your positive *I am* thoughts with love, the result will always be feelings of peace and joy. If you mix your negative *I am not* thoughts with fear, the result will be feelings such as anxiety and anger. These results can't be helped. What you mix together leads to a set result. If you want to change that result, or you desire a new feeling, you must change the ingredients. It's like mixing colors. You may want to make orange, but no matter how many times you mix blue with yellow, you'll keep producing green. Only once you mix red and yellow will you produce orange.

So many of us want peace and joy in our lives but can't seem to attain them. We don't know what we're doing wrong. Maybe we're afraid of failing, or of being criticized, so we keep telling ourselves, "I can't do that" or "I am not good enough" or "I am not [something]." Subconsciously, we are mixing the negative thoughts of *I am not* with fear-based emotions, which can only produce negative feelings. The only way to create positive feelings is to mix positive thoughts (I am) with positive emotions (love).

These feelings are what you project into the universe to create your experience of this world. Your feelings are the energy you project and the energy others feel from you. Others don't feel your thoughts; they feel your feelings. But your feelings result from a combination of your thoughts and emotions. So while positive thinking is good, it is not enough. Mix it with love, not fear, and then you will project the transformative power of your feelings into the universe.

AVOID YOUR KRYPTONITE

There is little Superman can't do. He has extraordinary powers, but he also has an Achilles heel: a piece of rock from his native planet, called kryptonite. Whenever he comes near this rock, he immediately feels weak. It's hard to imagine that a little piece of kryptonite could negate all his power, but it is a simple fact that this material does. You, too, have extraordinary powers that can be negated by your version of kryptonite.

In reality, there is little you can't do. Where do you get all your power? From the power of your *I am* presence. It enables you to attract all that you can dream into your life. It is the greatest mystical power of all. It is your connection to the Divine. With that power, nothing can stop you—if you don't let it.

But we all do. Your kryptonite activates when you say your *I am* statement out loud *before* you've affirmed it with yourself. Once you've declared your *I am* statement internally and know it to be true, it can never be taken away. But when you say it out loud before you have affirmed it internally, the kryptonite starts working. It slowly saps your strength. How? Others start to give you their opinions. "What are you talking about? You can't do that!" "You're not good enough!" As all this feedback from well-intentioned folks pours in, the kryptonite takes effect, and you start to doubt yourself. "What was I thinking? I'm not good enough for that."

What you had declared out loud in your *I am* statement is completely wiped out by what other people think your *I am* statement should be. Do you want to know what your *I am* statement will sound like if others complete it for you? "I am no good." "I am a loser." "I am . . ."—fill in the blank. That's not who you are, and you know it. Only you can complete your *I am* statement. Once you own that statement to be true, you can share it with others. But if you tell others what it is before you fully own it, you have given it away. It loses all its power. That is your kryptonite.

Once you know who you are and have repeated it internally a thousand times, then you can say it out loud. Then you can shout it from the rooftops because you will know it to be true. And when you know something to be true, no one can tell you anything that will make you believe otherwise. The only thing preventing you from being the person you want to be is you. You are already it. So say the silent "I am" and allow yourself to be it.

BE FIRST, DO SECOND

In the 1990s, Nike Inc. came out with an advertising slogan encouraging people to "Just Do It." The saying became remarkably popular. Why did it resonate so well? Because our society is filled with procrastinators. Nike challenged us to knock it off and "just do it." Brilliant. It motivated people to stop saying, "I'll do it later" and start to act now.

Procrastination is the feeling of non-alignment with your inner being. So your primary focus should be on that alignment, which will inevitably lead to inspired action. Being who you're capable of being will inspire you to do things that make a difference in how you feel, and this will help eliminate your procrastination. Being who you know you are will inspire you to do things to help achieve your desires. It will inspire you to serve. But *being* doesn't necessarily come from *doing*. A more appropriate slogan may be "Just Be It."

Don't get me wrong—it's great to be a doer. The world needs more people who get things done. Doing beats sitting around on a couch all day eating bonbons and watching old reruns on television. One of the reasons Nike's campaign was so successful is that we tend to give derogatory labels to people who don't get things done. There are those who talk a good game but never seem to accomplish anything and others who appear just plain lazy. We tell them (or at least think of saying), "Get off your butts and do something." My childhood friend Gregg Lorberbaum is a life coach who constantly tells his clients, "Always do what you say you are going to do."

Then there are people labeled "dreamers." We think their heads are in the clouds and they never actually apply themselves to getting something concrete done. But is it really so bad to be a dreamer? Shonda Rhimes, the brilliant scriptwriter and producer, told Dartmouth's graduating class of 2014 to "ditch the dream and be a doer, not a dreamer. . . . Just . . . do."[5] In one sense, she's absolutely right. Dreaming about something but never taking steps to make it happen doesn't help you get there. You'll become a person with a lot of dreams who never fulfilled their true potential. At the same time, running around "doing" without a well-defined direction won't get you very far. But what *is* your true potential? If you dream of doing something, own it first. *Be* it first. Know that you're already capable of achieving that dream. Allow the Law of Attraction to go to work with your intention. You will start to attract things into your life that will enable you to fulfill your dream. When those things then show up, act on them! Do what you need to get it done. The mantra is not "Be first, do never." It's "Be first, do second."

THE POWER OF DREAMS

We all have the power to dream. We can dream while we sleep, or we can dream while awake. We call the latter daydreaming. If you're going to daydream, make it count. It doesn't do you any good to think of wonderful things you'd like to achieve and then listen to that other voice in your head that says, "Yeah, but I can never do that." If you don't believe it to be true, it can't be true. You can't have one concept about who you are and then let it manifest as something else. If you don't believe you can ever do what you want or be who you want, then you can't, because your concept of yourself is always manifested in the physical world.

The flipside is that if you dream about what you want to achieve or the type of person you want to be, and you truly believe your dream will become reality, it can't fail to happen. It cannot not be true, and your life will begin to unfold so that you'll meet all the people you are supposed to meet, and you will do all the things you're supposed to do to turn that dream into your experience in the physical world.

When dreamers fail to get anything done, it's because they stopped believing they can. Believe in yourself, and when you dream, always assume the dream is already true. Dreaming about something or imagining it to be true doesn't mean you don't have to do anything. It just means you have to *be* it first. If you don't take this step, you may not know what to do to become what you imagined yourself to be.

Feel the Guidance of Your Higher Self

The real issue is not whether you are a doer. Abe Lincoln was a doer, but he still told us, "Whatever you are, be a good one."[6] The issue is: Who is telling you what to do? Are you taking instructions from the ego or from your Higher Self?

If your lower self is telling you to "go write that person a nasty email for what they did to you" or "go put that person out of business for trying to compete with you," it will not bring you peace and happiness. These sort of actions, motivated by fear and bitterness, are not productive. When we start with being who we really are, which is aligning with our Higher Self in the Present Room, then we are guided to "do" things that are productive and will bring us the peace and happiness we crave. Be first. Do second.

Your *I am* statement answers the question of who you are. Who you are is very different from whatever your job title is. Who you are as an expression of your Higher Power is the only question that matters. Your life experience changes when you make changes inside. Once you allow yourself to be who you are meant to be, your outer experience will change. Your job and responsibilities may not change, but your experience of them will. If we were to put them in the proper order of priority, it would start with being who you want to be and then doing what you want to do. Be first. Do second.

When you recognize that feeling of joy, when you are doing things you love, realize that you don't need to be "doing" anything in particular to access that feeling. That is conditional joy. You don't want to train your mind to believe you can feel good by doing certain things or by not doing other things. Your whole life would become a string of highs and lows, where your feelings depend on what action you are performing. Instead, allow yourself to feel that joy no matter what you're doing. That is unconditional joy. If you access your joy by just being your best self, and not by doing a particular action, then you can feel it any time.

The one thing the mystics have been telling us since the beginning of time is to awaken. This awareness of your true being in all moments is one form of waking up to your Higher Self. If you can do just one thing, it should be to wake up. Why do anything else? This is your ticket to enlightenment. There is only one problem: To awaken is to become aware. So you can't *do* it;

you can only *be* it. To be awake is to be aware of your oneness with all things. To be awake is to be aware of which room your thoughts are in. To be awake is to be aware of which movie you are watching.

THE INTERNAL MIRROR

Observe your behavior as you are reading this book right now. Visualize a video camera in the corner of the room. Now imagine watching yourself through that camera as you are reading. You are observing yourself and your own behavior. This is much like looking in a mirror. You see a reflection of yourself, but that reflection is your external self. The mirror and the camera don't show what you are like inside.

What if there were such a thing as an internal mirror? What if you could look in a mirror and feel exactly what you're like inside? Would you feel anger, guilt, fear, or anxiety? Or would you feel love, joy, and compassion? If you looked within the internal mirror, into the purity of your heart, would you feel at peace? Ultimately, the external mirror reflects how people perceive you on the outside, while the internal mirror reflects how people perceive you on the inside.

There are a lot of people who look in an external mirror and like what they see. But would all of them be just as comfortable looking in an internal mirror and feeling what they are like on the inside? On the other hand, aren't there many wonderful people who don't seem very comfortable with what they see in the external mirror but would enjoy looking in the internal mirror? The real question is, which is more important to you?

THE FEELING OF PAIN

There are similarities between our internal and external selves. The physical body is an amazing instrument. For instance, suppose you get a cut or burn. Your body tells you that you're hurt by causing you to feel pain in the affected area, or you may see a mark on your skin. Then your body's miraculous self-healing mechanism takes over and begins the healing process. Over time, you no longer feel the pain or see the burn.

Your mind is an amazing instrument as well. If someone does something you perceive as an attack, you feel hurt. You say, "He really hurt my feelings" or "She wounded me." You feel pain inside, just as you felt pain on the outside when you got a burn. You may wonder how that's possible. Yet often the level of pain we feel inside is significantly greater than what we feel on the outside. In both cases, though, what we feel helps us recognize how much we have been hurt.

What you feel tells you what is wrong on the outside *and* inside. Similarly, the feelings we create inside are reflected in the world around us and inside of us. This was beautifully illustrated in the extraordinary documentary *Heal* by Kelly Noonan Gores.[7] With the help of gifted doctors and scientists such as Dr. Bruce Lipton, Dr. Joe Dispenza, and Gregg Braden, the film presents some fascinating research and evidence on how our thoughts and emotions have tremendous healing powers, even for life-threatening autoimmune diseases. As with a cut or burn, we experience miraculous healing by the cells in our bodies because we expect them to heal. But what if we mixed intention with emotions to heal parts of our bodies that we didn't think could be healed? If our cells can heal a cut or burn all on their own, why shouldn't they be able to heal any ailment in our body all by themselves? We are now learning that this is not only possible, but it is happening all around us. Miraculous healings took place centuries ago. Science is finally starting to be able to explain them.

It becomes all the more important to recognize that our feelings are the creative force that creates what we see in the physical world, including our bodies. If we look in the external mirror and all we see is our physical body, we will go through this life only seeing others' physical bodies. As we judge our own looks in the mirror, we will go around judging everyone else's, too. But if we see the beautiful attributes we possess inside, that's what we will see when we look at everyone else. This in turn strengthens our compassion for others, which is our path to serenity.

But focusing on our feelings and internal characteristics is not intuitively what we do. Our society is extremely "looks" conscious, which ironically means it is unconscious. This is nothing new. As the Bible says: "For the Lord seeth not as a man seeth, for man looketh on the outward appearance, but the Lord looketh on the heart" (Samuel 16:7).[8] The fact is that there is no separate internal mirror; there's only a physical mirror, and it is your choice whether you see your outward appearance or your heart when you look in that mirror. Next time you pass a mirror, decide for yourself which image you're going to see—your external self or your internal self. If you see your outward appearance, you are looking at the external mirror. If you feel your heart, you are looking at the internal mirror.

PERFECTION

When we look in the external mirror, we see our physical body in all its perfection and perceived imperfections. No matter what is reflected, we are constantly told no one is perfect. But our eternal being is perfect, and in any moment that we are perfectly aligned with it, then we are perfect too.

In the movie *Friday Night Lights*, Billy Bob Thornton plays the coach of an undefeated high school football team losing at halftime of the state championship game.[9] Instead of screaming at his players to fire them up and keep their perfect record intact, his message to them is that the final score is not the indicator for whether they stay perfect. It's about the relationship they maintain with each other and the relationship they maintain with themselves.

We don't each have to be perfect for the world to be perfect. The world can be perfectly made up of everyone's imperfections. But if we are all made in the likeness of our Creator, who is perfect, doesn't that make us all perfect, too? The world is perfect. The stars, the galaxies—it's all perfect. That's all you need to know. Life is perfect, as it should be, because nothing real ever changes. When living things die and grow again in infinite cycles, this is just what we can see. Our bodies, too, are perfect in their creation, with every cell working in perfect harmony. You are perfect and your neighbor is perfect. We're all perfect. Still, that does not mean we all act perfectly all the time.

The problem is that we forget who we are. We spend too much time listening to our lower self instead of our Higher Self. If it were possible to reprogram ourselves so that all our thoughts, words, and actions were in harmony with our eternal being, then we would be truly perfect all the time. So, what's stopping us? In the Present Room, all our thoughts, words, and actions are in harmony with our Higher Power. In the Present Room, we have a reverence for all things that are good. We continuously put the higher good of all over the perceived good of our selves.

The only thing preventing you from recognizing your perfection is you—not the you that experiences your connection with the Divine, but the you that thinks it is separate from the very Source that created you. If you think about it, it's silly. All the trillions of cells in your body function perfectly with each other because they know they're all part of the same entity. But the billions of people on this planet can't function perfectly with each other because they think they are separate from the whole. At what point did we separate? At what point did we disconnect from the Source that created us? The birth of a child is a perfect process. At what age does a child stop being perfect? This shift to "imperfection" happens when our ego, fed by the outside world, tells us we're not perfect. Then if we listen carefully, our creator responds by telling us, "You are perfect just the way you are."

The recognition of our own perfection depends on which voice we listen to, which also determines which room we're in. In the Past Room, you hear a voice that says, "It was his fault." In the Future Room, you hear a voice that says, "You're not good enough for that." In the Present Room, you hear a voice that says, "You are perfect, just the way you are."

I AM IN YOU

What is our *I am* presence? This presence can be described as our "God Self," but really it is part of us that is not our physical body. People of different faiths call it different things, but what does it matter what it's called? You can't see it; you can only feel it. If you believe "That is who I am," then that is what it is. If you believe "I am my finite body," then that is what will be true for you. If you believe you are an infinite soul made in the image of God, then that is what you are.

In the Hindu faith, they call the inner soul the atman, which is the mirror image of Brahman, or God. As a practitioner of that faith, your goal is the realization that you are that soul and not your physical body. Taking it one step further is the concept of Advaita, which is the realization that you are Brahman. As you awaken, you are joined with this consciousness of unity, or non-duality. You are, in essence, saying, "I am you" to that presence, or to all that there is. When you enter this consciousness, you recognize your oneness with both Brahman and atman. They are one. You are one with them. Hence, they are saying to you, "I am you."

It's interesting that there is always so much focus on the differences between Christianity and other faiths, when the similarities are enormous. The Holy Spirit is the Christian term for that part of us that is not our body. Like the Hindus recognizing the atman, or the Jews' recognition of *neshama*, the realization of the Holy Spirit within us is a vital step for those of the Christian faith. When you step into the Present Room, you realize you're not a separate body, but rather you are connected to the Divine via the Holy Spirit. As Jesus says in the New Testament (John 14:20),

"On that day, you will realize that I am in my Father, and you are in me, and I am in you."[10] Christ could not be any clearer in his message that we are all connected. When you feel that connection, it is clear we are not the separate bodies we see walking around. When you feel that connection, you are perfectly aligned with the Holy Spirit. When you feel that connection, you are in the Present Room.

CHAPTER 8

Going Back Home

BECAUSE WE BELIEVE WE ARE SEPARATE FROM GOD, WE FEEL lost. Without our connection to the Divine, we can't help but feel like we don't know our way back home. Home is where we feel connected to our Source, where we are guided by our Higher Power and feel only love. Home is where God is. Home is the Present Room. Instead of trying to do everything we can to get home, we tend to run in the opposite direction. Instead of being drawn to the light, most of us are blinded by the light and turn away.

As seventeenth-century mystic Meister Eckhart said, "God is at home. It is we who have gone out for a walk."[1] Subconscious guilt is a big reason for us leaving God behind. It can make us feel unworthy of God because of the separation we have placed between God and us. As a result, home has become a terrifying place for us to go. Walking into the Present Room and greeting all the ascended masters is a frightening prospect. *What will they think? Do I really belong here? They are perfect and I am not.* It is so much easier to hang out in the Past Room, wallow in our own guilt, and project it on to others.

We can't let our fears get in the way of our journey to the Divine. It takes a few brave souls to start the process, and then everyone begins to follow—slowly at first, and then it starts to accelerate. One bright light can illuminate a thousand dark souls. But you can't force people to go home. If you make the journey home first, your light will shine, and many others will follow. When we live in the Present Room and watch the Present Movie, others will want to sit in the same theater.

FOLLOW YOUR INTERNAL GPS

GPS is one of the greatest human inventions. You push a button in your car that says "go home," and it directs you there. However dark or cloudy or miserable it is outside, the GPS's algorithm doesn't care. It's immune to the dark. It tells you every turn you need to make, and not only does it show you a map of how to get home, the device speaks to you! When you veer off course because you weren't paying attention, it says, "Recalculating" and figures out where you are after the screw up. Then, without any criticism, it gives you new directions home.

Well, the great news is that we have an internal GPS that can tell us exactly how to get home. Our built-in GPS is also called many things, such as Holy Spirit, Divine consciousness, Higher Self, and more. It doesn't matter how lost you get or how dark and miserable you think your life is; your internal GPS always knows where you are and how to get you back home. There is never just one route to take, either. Every time you go off course, it recalculates to show you many paths you can take, and all paths lead back to the same place—home.

How do you turn on this internal GPS? Simply sit down in a quiet place, close your eyes, and say, "Okay, here I am. Show me the way to go home." Ironically, the answer you will get is "You are already there." Because home is the Present Room, and when you realize, *I am here*, you are realizing you are home. The best depiction of this concept comes at the end of *The Wizard of Oz*, when Glinda the Good Witch tells Dorothy that she could have gone home anytime she wanted to. When she clicks her heels three times, she awakens from the dream. Does she wake up in a new paradise? No. She wakes up on the same poor farm where she'd always lived, but now her experience of being on that farm feels completely different. Instead of frustration, fear, and a desire to run away, she is filled with appreciation, joy, and love. Her physical body never left the farm, just her fearful thoughts. When once she lived in the Future Room, she finally awakens in the Present Room.

Besides GPS, there are also countless maps that can help you find your way home if you are lost. They have many names, such as the *Bible*, the *Torah*, the *Quran*, and the *Bhagavad-Gita*. You can even find clues in popular culture such as the movie *Terminator 2*. In this film, Arnold Schwarzenegger plays the role of a human-like machine who comes to Earth knowing both where he came from and why he has come here: to protect a young man named John Conner. His time on Earth is totally devoted to that mission. Unwavering. Fully committed. Although he's here physically, he knows he is just visiting this planet for a short time.

Isn't that the same for all of us? Whether you like it or not, you are just visiting this planet for a short time. What is your mission here? What do you want to accomplish before you go back home?

The *Kabbalah*, which is the mystical aspect of Judaism, essentially teaches that our mission here is to find our way back to the creator by aligning our intentions with the creator's intentions. We all need to remember where we came from and why we are here and devote our time on Earth to that mission. Nothing else matters.

When you remember who you are, and you know where you are, your experience of life alters radically. This is because you are in the place you are supposed to be: the Present Room. That's home base, the place you will stay—except when you don't. Because until you completely align yourself with your inner being, you will continually forget who you are and find yourself far from home. It is like walking around with amnesia or sleepwalking. The good news is that as long as you constantly check where you are, you will find your way home again.

USING YOUR INTERNAL GPS

The one thing we need for our internal GPS to work is trust. When we click on the GPS in our car, we follow the GPS's directions, assuming it will take us where we want to go. We don't turn it on and worry that it's taking us to the wrong place. Damn, I put in New Jersey and it took me to Delaware! On the contrary, we have complete confidence we will reach our destination. We have trust in the GPS, or the smartphone app that we use, so we can sit back and enjoy the ride.

Having trouble turning on your internal GPS? I know, there's no instruction manual. Start by saying to yourself, "Here I am. I know where I want to go, but I don't know how to get there. Show me the way!" Trust in your Higher Power, that quiet voice inside you. The loud voice is the ego, and it is always screaming from the back seat, trying to give you bad directions. Listen to the quiet voice. It is the one in the front seat, right next to you. It always knows how to get you where you would like to be, in the least amount of time—especially when that place is home, where you find peace, love, and tranquility. Home is in the Present Room, and you can go back whenever you want. So turn on your internal GPS and let it take you there.

You also need to know where you want to go. You can't say, "Get me there" without entering a destination. The tool you use for that is your imagination. Simply imagine where you would like to be in your life. Picture in your mind that you are already there, and feel it in your heart. Give a little thanks to your Source for allowing you to be there, and then follow your internal GPS, trusting it will take you where you imagined yourself to be.

THE AMERICAN DREAM

We all seem to be searching for something. For Monty Python, it was the Holy Grail. For Indiana Jones, it was the Lost Ark. For a large portion of our population, it's the American Dream. What is the American Dream, anyway? It varies for everyone, but it mostly seems to mean a high level of monetary wealth and an equally high dose of relaxation and comfort. Win the lotto—jackpot! You can quit your job and live a life of leisure. But if you don't strike it rich, you're doomed to a lifetime of hard labor, unable to enjoy the benefits of those appearing on the *Lifestyles of the Rich and Famous.*

What is our preoccupation with external rather than internal wealth? We have already established that accumulating more stuff doesn't necessarily make us happy, and many times the path to accumulating more stuff isn't an enjoyable one. Yet still we bust our butts and delay gratification until we have made it in the world. Then, and only then, can we enjoy our hard-earned riches.

Delayed gratification—what a misunderstood term. Why wait until some future time to enjoy life when you can enjoy it right now? That is not to say you should stop working hard at what you do, but you don't have to wait until later to enjoy the present moment. Step into the Present Room now. You are already living the American Dream. This idea can't be illustrated any better than by the parable of the Mexican fisherman who meets the ambitious American investment banker.[2] The author is unknown, but it goes something like this:

An American investment banker was taking a much-needed vacation in a coastal Mexican village, when a small boat with just one fisherman docked. The boat had several large fresh fish in it.

The investment banker was impressed by the quality of the fish and asked the Mexican how long it took to catch them.

The Mexican replied, "Only a little while."

The banker then asked why he didn't stay out longer and catch more fish.

The Mexican fisherman replied that he had enough to support his family's immediate needs.

The American then asked, "But what do you do with the rest of your time?"

The Mexican fisherman replied, "I sleep late, fish a little, play with my children, take *siesta* with my wife, and stroll into the village each evening, where I sip wine and play guitar with my *amigos*. I have a full and busy life, *señor*."

The investment banker scoffed. "I have an Ivy League MBA, and I could help you. You could spend more time fishing and with the proceeds buy a bigger boat, and with the proceeds from the bigger boat, you could buy several boats until eventually you would have a whole fleet of fishing boats. Instead of selling your catch to the middleman, you could sell directly to the processor, eventually opening your own cannery. You could control the product, processing, and distribution."

Then he added, "Of course, you would need to leave this small village and move to Mexico City, where you would run your growing enterprise."

The Mexican fisherman asked, "But, *señor*, how long will this all take?"

To which the American replied, "Fifteen to twenty years."

"But what then?"

The American laughed. "That's the best part. When the time is right, you would announce an IPO and sell your company stock to the public and become very rich. You could make millions."

"Millions, *señor*? Then what?"

To which the investment banker replied, "Then you would retire. You could move to a small coastal village where you would sleep late, fish a little, play with your kids, take *siesta* with your wife, and stroll to the village in the evenings, where you could sip wine and play guitar with your *amigos*."

When our thoughts are in the Past Room, we get very jealous of what other people have. All we can think about is why we don't have what they have. When our thoughts are in the Future Room, we can't stop thinking about what we want to get. When our thoughts are in the Present Room, we appreciate everything we have. Instead of looking for things outside of us to bring us the peace and joy we crave, we realize we don't need to "get" anything to feel that very peace and joy. We can either take the long road to get there, as the investment banker suggests, or take the short road. We don't need to go anywhere before we come back home. We just need to realize we are already there.

SILENCING THE *WHAT IFS*

Two words that bring us instantly into the Past Room are *what if*, as in *What if I hadn't sent that email?* We beat ourselves up with *what if*s, and every time we do, our thoughts go right back to the Past Room. *What if I didn't go there that night? What if I hadn't said those things to her?* How can one regrettable thing we say or do dictate our experience of life going forward? Because we keep holding on to it. As we keep reliving it, it keeps controlling us. The longer we stay in the Past Room, the longer we deprive ourselves of the peace of the Present Room. But we don't have to. The problem is that we do something, we regret it, and then we rehash it in our mind over and over. So how do we get our lives back on track and move back to the Present Room? By forgiving ourselves for anything we have said or done and refocusing our thoughts on the present moment. This will allow the future life events to unfold in the Present Room.

Any time we start focusing on *what if* scenarios, we inevitably compare our current situation to what *could* be. Usually we believe our life would have turned out much better in the *what if* scenario. But does it really make a difference? Our physical life may change over the short term, but if we maintain our alignment with our eternal being, what if we all end up in the same place anyway?

We all have *what if* experiences, moments we would like to do over. Instead of beating ourselves up over what we did, *à la* living in the Past Room, we just need to move into the Present Room, and we'll end up where we wanted to be in the first place. We don't know what life situations we're supposed to experience. We tend to assume that if a particular event hadn't happened, we would never have had to experience the outcome of that event, but this is not necessarily true.

Sometimes it helps to witness a *what if* scenario being played out. One of the best illustrations of this is the 1998 movie *Sliding Doors*.[3] It chronicles the life of a character played by Gwyneth Paltrow following two different paths. After being fired from her job, she goes down to the London Underground to take a train home, and the sliding doors shut in her face. Having just missed the train, she sits on the stairs, probably thinking, "What if I'd made that train?" The rest of the movie tracks two parallel lives for her character. In one, we see how her life unfolds after missing the train. In the other, we see what would have happened if she'd caught the train. She encounters a completely different series of experiences on each path, but they both lead her to meet the same man she would fall in love with.

What if *Sliding Doors* depicted what goes on every day? What if we are all living parallel possibilities of the same life? It's not hard to imagine. Just think of what your life would be like right now if you hadn't taken one particular action, or if you had said yes to something you really wanted, instead of passing on it due to fearful thoughts. What if you forgave that person instead of seeking revenge? What if you followed your own heart, instead of listening to the opinions of others? There are multiple paths our lives can travel at any point in time, and the path we experience is the one led by the emotions we feel.

A Course in Miracles teaches us that for every person there is a wholly individualized curriculum. Your Higher Power is at work in your life with a plan much bigger and better than yours. Recognize when you are trying to force something to happen, and instead allow your life to unfold in alignment with your Higher Power's plan. Whatever happens in this physical life provides lessons we need to learn. If the lesson doesn't present itself in one physical encounter, it may appear in another. If we don't learn the lesson presented to us, don't worry; it will keep coming back in different forms until we finally comprehend it. You are always doing something—but you could be doing something else. Every moment of your life you are making decisions, and there are countless choices you could make, each taking your life in a different direction. Sometimes the choice is as small as the route you take home from the grocery store. Sometimes it's as big as a career change. But despite the varying levels of magnitude, each decision you make takes your life in a slightly different direction. So start to watch the decisions you make every day. Think *what if* you took that other path—but instead of trying to figure out which path you should take, simply imagine where you want to be. Mix that image with love, and then feel your way down the path that allows that image to come to life. As the mystic Neville Goddard puts it, "Every state is already there as 'mere possibilities' as long as we think of them, but as overpoweringly real when we think from them."

CREATING PARALLEL SCRIPTS

Shonda Rhimes has created some of the most memorable shows on primetime television. Two of my favorites are *Grey's Anatomy* and *Private Practice*, which my wife and I would watch every week. In *Grey's Anatomy*, she took a bunch of young interns and wove their personal and professional lives together over the course of more than a decade. There was triumph and disappointment, heartache and joy. The stories contain the entire gamut of emotions. How are those episodes different from the daily scenes in the movie of our life? One difference is that the actors have to follow a specific script. Rhimes (or her team) wrote it, and they couldn't alter it. That, however, is not how our lives unfold.

Imagine that Shonda Rhimes is creating a new television show and writes countless scripts for each episode. Now imagine there is an interactive way to watch each episode, where the script you see acted out on the television coincides with the thoughts in your mind and the feelings in your heart at the time you're watching the show. You come home from work upset after a tough day, still mad at a coworker, and the episode you watch is full of angry people and revenge. The next time you watch, you've just started dating someone new and your heart is singing with joy. What a surprise—the episode you watch that night is full of joy and the message of love.

Are your feelings creating the episode you are watching? No! Rhimes already created the show. Your emotions just determine which version of the episode you watch today. Just like yesterday's show and tomorrow's show—they're all different, determined by how you feel at the time, but they've already been created.

The same goes for your experience of life. Everything you can imagine doing has already been done. You just haven't experienced it yet because your thoughts and emotions have sent you on a completely different vibrational frequency from the one that particular experience of life requires from you. But just because you are not experiencing it today, that doesn't mean you can't experience it tomorrow. It's always there. You just can't get there by continuing to focus on the concerns you're currently focusing on. You can only get there by changing the frequency of your thoughts and emotions.

Which movie theater are you in, and which scene in your life movie are you watching right now? The script is up to you. As soon as you can imagine it, your eternal being has written a script for the movie of your life. You don't have to *make* it happen; you just have to *allow* it to happen.

If you took all the episodes of *Grey's Anatomy* and put them in order, they would take you from when the characters were interns at the hospital to when they became accomplished doctors. If you go back and watch one of the earlier episodes, you already know how things will turn out. You see Meredith Gray, played by Ellen Pompeo, going through many trials, tribulations, tragedies, and joyful events. During each episode, she is engrossed in what is happening at that time. But because you've already watched the last episode, you know she will achieve her goal of becoming an accomplished surgeon. She is already a doctor, even if she can't yet see it at the start of the series.

Our everyday lives work the same way. I was always intrigued with the mystics and wished I could become one. Eventually, I realized nobody has to do anything to become a mystic. We already are mystics. We just have to undo a whole lot of un-mystic behavior we learned from others who have yet to undo their acquired behavior. As of this moment, I know I am a mystic author, even while I'm commuting into New York City every day to work for a global investment bank before this book is published. I don't know how each episode in my life will turn out, but I know how the series of my life will unfold. Every day, I envision myself as a mystic author, and I know I will become one at some point in my human experience.

Every day you wake up to a new episode in the story of your life. You are the star in 365 different episodes every year, and since there is no cancellation policy, your contract runs until the day you leave this physical plane. The show goes on, whether you're aware of it or not. So as soon as you awaken in the morning, you can consciously decide which theater you're going to watch this episode from. If you find yourself thinking about yesterday's episode as soon as you wake up, it will likely generate similar emotions, and old patterns of behavior will continue to pop up during the day. When this happens, you are sitting in the Past Theater watching reruns in the story of your life.

Remember that certain scripts only play in certain theaters. It doesn't work to imagine a wonderful script for your life movie, full of abundance and joy, but then try to watch it in the Past Theater. The episode you imagined is all cued up and ready to play in the Present Theater. You just need to step in, take your seat, and start watching.

THE PRODIGAL SON

The parable of the prodigal son is the story of the lost son who finds his way back home.[4] In this biblical story told by Jesus, a man had two sons. One day, the youngest son asked to receive his inheritance now, and his father complied. After he went off and spent his entire inheritance, he found himself working as a poor hired servant far away from home. Eventually, he decided to go back to his father and beg for forgiveness, hoping to work for his father as a hired servant because he felt he was no longer worthy of being called his son. Much to his surprise, his father ran to greet him when he returned home, celebrating his son's return.

What does this really mean? Did Jesus want to tell us the story of some random kid who decided to run off to the big city one day and then came home when all his money ran out? Or was he trying to illustrate a much larger lesson, of how we can all get lost for a while, but our father will always welcome us back?

The "running away" in this parable is more metaphorical than it is literal. Squandering our inheritance is the same as forgetting our connection to our Source. The son left and went to another room and stepped back through the Present Door. He left the Present Room and then found his way back. When the prodigal son finally found his way home, the door wasn't locked. This shows us that the door is always open. We are always welcome back home. It is not our Higher Power or God the Father who keeps us out. It is our own subconscious guilt. We come up with all kinds of excuses for why we can't face the light, but they always stem from the same source—our own fears.

Jesus spoke in parables so he could be better understood by his followers. If he had started talking about metaphysics the way Deepak Chopra does, he would have received a lot of blank stares. He probably got a lot of blank stares anyway, but his parables were a little less intimidating for the people of those times. The expression "I was lost but now I'm found" means "I was in the wrong room and didn't know it. But then I found my way home, which is right here in the Present Room, the same place we end up after we leave this physical plane."

I remember when my dad knew he had a failing heart and only a few months to live—he promised he would look after me and our family after he passed away. A few months later, I looked up to the heavens and started asking him questions. "Where are you, Father? Where did you go?" After silent contemplation, his response was always the same: "I am right here. I never went anywhere." What a surprise. That's the same place God is—and Buddha, and Brahman, and Moses, and Jesus, too. They are all right here with us. They never went anywhere either.

Having been blessed with two beautiful Jewish girls in my life, my wife and my daughter, I find Hebrew mysticism especially intriguing. *Neshama* is the Hebrew word for soul, or spirit. In the Jewish faith, it is believed that when you fulfill your purpose here on Earth, your soul can go back home. My father-in-law, Sheldon Kolinsky, was truly a *neshama*. He was one of the kindest souls I ever met. He saw the good in everything. He didn't need an expensive steak dinner to appreciate the food. If you made him a hamburger, he would say it was the best burger he'd ever had in his life. He also loved people. Wherever he went, he walked away knowing something personal about everyone he came in contact with. He seemed to have a unique ability to strike a chord in them. Everyone remembered him and loved him. He embodied the consciousness of nonduality; he looked at everyone else as one with him. If a *neshama* is one who fulfills his purpose here on Earth and then goes home, then Sheldon has clearly found his way back home.

Both my father and my father-in-law spent much of their time in the Present Room. Although they were raised in different faiths, they both had a connection to God the Father. That doesn't mean they never forgot that Divine connection, but whenever they did, they were always welcomed back home with open arms. We are always welcomed back into the Present Room by our eternal being, who has never left.

CHAPTER 9

STAYING ON THE PATH

THE PRIMARY GOAL OF SPIRITUAL PATHS IS TO REMIND US OF our connection to our Source. The Divine amnesia we suffer from has allowed us to slip into a dream and imagine we are separate from each other in this Land of Perception and Time that we call our physical reality. Being on the spiritual path means waking up from that dream. But, instead of fully awakening, most of us settle for little glimpses of enlightenment, and then we go back to our daily routine. When our lives become challenging enough, we reach inside for a little help, and we typically find some comfort. But it's short-lived. Why? We don't *stay* on the path. We convince ourselves that enlightenment is reserved for the seers who spend their lives meditating in caves. Most people believe following the spiritual path is impractical in the "real world." This is not true!

Awakening to our awareness of Divine consciousness takes some serious contemplation, but you don't have to be isolated on some far-off hilltop to carry out your contemplative practice. You can do it in every moment of your everyday life. You can observe your thoughts, behavior, and feelings throughout the day in a multitude of ways, from the time you begin your commute in the morning until you fall asleep at night. It's challenging to find your inner guide when you're busy living your life, but it's doable.

People often hear about the importance of meditation, inner reflection, contemplation, and the like, and they immediately respond, "I know, I know, it's important, but it's easy for you to do. I'm crazy busy." Well guess what: Your life will not stop being crazy busy in order to give you time to connect with your Source within. Instead, you have to find ways to connect to that Divine presence *during* your busy life. When you do—and you *can*—then your busy life will become, oh, so much more enjoyable!

MEDITATION

Few activities are better at getting us back on the spiritual path than meditation. Meditation is a key to making our connection to the Divine, and there are many helpful tools available for all practitioners. Michael Acton Smith and Alex Tew wrote an insightful book, *Calm*, which has valuable tips for raising your awareness of mindfulness.

Still, meditation doesn't have to be done in isolation. It can and must be done anywhere—and right now. Smith and Tew also created the Calm app to teach the practice of mindful meditation anywhere that you use a mobile device. If you find a quiet place and can listen to the "7 Days of Calm," you should.[1]

Even without apps, we can meditate any time in our lives; we just need to alter our perception of what meditation is. Meditation is choosing which room you want to be in by focusing on the stillness in the spaces between thoughts. Our thoughts are what pull us out of the Present Room, and since meditation is the absence of thought, it is the quickest way to bring us back there. Meditation begins as soon as you start watching the Present Movie, because when you start observing your life from the perspective of the observer, you have already separated your awareness from your thoughts. As Raul Julia, the extraordinary actor and humanitarian, once said, "We tend to think of meditation in only one way. But life itself is a meditation."[2]

SIMPLE VS. EASY

I have used the words "simple" and "simply" many times in this book. Although I have tried to simplify complex ideas, this doesn't mean they are easy to practice. I could tell you *simply* to break up my concrete driveway into little pieces and load all the chunks on to a truck. Simple to say. Hard to do. If we show someone our new smartphone, we *simply* show them the basic functionality. We say, "Look at my pictures" or "Look at this cool app" or "Look at the clarity of my screen." We don't go into detail about the technical design of the phone because people wouldn't understand what we're saying. We just demonstrate the phone's usefulness in a way they can comprehend. Metaphysical principles are no different. I have tried to explain these principles in an accessible way, so they can be applied more consistently in your life.

To keep it simple: The world is a living, breathing organism, and we are all vibrational beings who can affect the world in and around us with our thoughts and emotions.

GROWING UP

What is the one thing you can do by being but not by doing?

Grow.

We all hope to grow into the person we want to become—to grow into the person we already are—but just don't know how yet. We've all seen glimpses of that awesome person inside of us, and these moments made us feel good. We've also seen the not-so-awesome side of ourselves, which hasn't made us feel good inside. Regardless, we can't wait to grow into that person we want to be. We view it as getting from Point A to Point B, with Point A being the person we are now and Point B being the person we want to become. We also think we have to do many things to get to Point B. But we can't *do* anything to grow; we can only *allow* ourselves to grow. No one can help us. We can't rush it, either. In reality, we are already at Point B; we just don't realize it yet.

When my siblings and I were kids, our friends down the block had an apple tree and a cherry tree in their backyard. Every year by late summer, the ripe cherries started to fall off the tree, and we picked them up and brought them home so my mother could make cherry pies. She always baked two pies, one for us and one for the Montgomerys. Then the apples would fall off the tree. Once again, we collected all the fruit and brought it home. Our mom turned these into two incredible apple pies. But in the winter, when we had a craving for those pies, we couldn't go into the Montgomerys' backyard and say, "Grow!" to the trees. We couldn't speed up the process. We had to let them be and grow new fruit at their own pace. But we always knew what the outcome would be. Each spring they flowered, and each fall they never failed to produce more apples and cherries. Those trees always contained the essence of what they produced. Although we couldn't see the apples in the winter, they were always there.

It's the same with people. If you imagine yourself to be something, you have to allow yourself to grow into that something at the right pace. Even if others can't see it yet, you never stop being it once you imagine it to be true.

NATURE GETS IT

Have you ever seen trees argue with each other? Have you ever seen a mountain get up and move because it didn't like the mountain next to it? Have you ever seen the sun set in the east because it got tired of setting in the west? We humans do these things all the time. We argue and fight with each other. We get up and move when we don't like our neighbor anymore. We might change our routines because we get bored.

How about emotions? Does a flower worry it is getting too wet from the rain? No, but we do. We worry about everything. No wonder the average lifespan of a person is 75 years and the average lifespan of a tree is 150 years. The tree doesn't worry. Nature doesn't worry.

We can learn so much from nature if we just take the time to do so. Nature teaches us that the pace of what goes on outside us is uncorrelated with our inner pace. Some of the world's greatest writers and poets understood this concept. They called themselves transcendentalists: extraordinary humans like Henry Wadsworth Longfellow, Emily Dickinson, and Ralph Waldo Emerson. They devoted much of their lives to understanding the lessons nature tries to share with us. They taught us that inspiration comes from within.

Humans are different from the rest of nature in the sense that the natural world unfolds and connects with no resistance, yet we constantly put up roadblocks to the experience of oneness with all living things. *A Course in Miracles* calls this "blocks to the awareness of love's presence."[3] Your thinking is what puts up these barriers, and only an absence of thinking will remove them. When you focus your thoughts in the Past or Future Room, you have in effect put up blocks to the awareness of love's presence. When you focus on the space between the thoughts and move into the Present Room, your absence of thinking allows you to experience your oneness with all things. You have essentially removed the blocks to love's awareness by removing the thoughts that erected the blocks in the first place. If you slow down and feel the love inside, you will connect to your Divine presence, no matter what your surroundings.

Nature is a helpful stimulant to remind you of your connection to all living things, but it is not the only way for you to realize that connection. Millions of people commute to work in big cities on roads, railways, and sidewalks—not exactly nature trails. If you commute, you have to find other ways to connect to your Source. In fact, as I write this sentence, I'm stuck on a jam-packed commuter train with people agitated because the train is not moving. Many people are starting to feel anxiety as they leave their comfort zone and flood into the Future Room. If you can smile and find peace in this situation, then you can move into the Present Room in just about any situation. Of course, it would be much easier to find peace if you were walking around in nature, but that can't be an excuse. Learn to find peace in the challenging situations. Then, whenever you get the opportunity to go out into nature, it will amplify your feeling of connection to all.

Nature is also about beauty. It is the most natural form of beauty because there is no judgment; it just *is*. If you visit a place like Bryce Canyon or Zion National Park in Southern Utah and look out over the cliffs at the majestic mountain tops, the beauty will take your breath away. Nature has such a profound impact on us because we recognize the inherent beauty of it. It consumes us, and we can't help but feel it. The feeling is universal. Every sunset is unique and every sunset is beautiful. Every person is unique and every person is beautiful too. Why aren't we uplifted in the same way by every human we meet? Because we don't recognize the inherent beauty in them. We judge other people all the time, but we rarely judge nature. It's as simple as that.

But there is even more to it. Sunsets don't worry about being beautiful. People do. Sunsets don't get together with each other after they go down and say things like, "Darn, I really didn't look good today. I hope there weren't many people looking at me." There is no doubt in their inherent beauty. People watching the sunsets don't usually say, "Wow, this sunset is pretty lame. The one yesterday was much better." They just appreciate it for the beautiful thing it is.

If people were more like the rest of nature and simply recognized the beauty within themselves, they would project that beauty on to others. Likewise, if we viewed other people the way we view nature, without judgment, we would recognize the inherent beauty in all human beings. We are capable of both. It starts with the recognition "I am beautiful." This isn't hard to do once you recognize you were created from the same Source as the rest of nature. God didn't go around saying, "Okay, let me make this flower beautiful . . . and let me make this guy ugly." The flower, the guy, and you are made of the same stuff. When you finally recognize that, you start to understand that not only are you beautiful but so is every other person. In other words, as you learn to see the beauty in yourself, so you will see the beauty in others.

Your Mantra Is Your Reminder

In addition to meditation, reciting mantras that resonate with you and move you to take your life to another level are also empowering. Even if you find peace in your life or are pretty content, the feeling is fleeting: It can last for hours, and sometimes days, but rarely does it last longer. Life gets in the way. You return to your old routine, thinking it's a rat race out there, and even when you think back to the time you read something that struck a chord, you are no longer playing that tune.

But a mantra serves as a daily, or moment-to-moment, reminder of who we really are. You'd be hard-pressed to find a mystic who has not developed their own mantra or personal prayer that immediately brings them to a state of peace. For Christians, it may be the Lord's Prayer; for Hindus, it may be the *Vedanta-sutras*; and for Jews, it may be *The Shema*. People respond to words differently. There are many mantras and prayers, and at least one of them will resonate deep inside you. You just have to discover it. The only thing preventing you from experiencing the benefit of a personal mantra is not taking the time to find one.

For me, a daily mantra from *A Course in Miracles* immediately reconnects me to the Divine. It encompasses the principles of the present moment, surrender, trust in your Higher Power, knowing, and peace. The same message has been repeated in various forms over and over for ages. We just don't keep it at the forefront of our minds. Its effectiveness lies in its simplicity. Here's the twenty-three-word mantra from *A Course in Miracles*, Lesson 365: "This Holy Instant would I give to you. Be you in charge for I will follow. Certain your direction will give me peace."[4]

These words express the simple recognition of a higher Source that takes your thoughts from the Past or Future Room and brings them back into the Present Room. This is why the first three words of the mantra are so crucial. "This Holy Instant" doesn't mean tomorrow, yesterday, or "when I get around to it." It means right now, in the present. You are saying to yourself, "Get me in the right room, now." The next five words, "which I give to you," are about surrender. To surrender to a higher Source, you first need to be aware that there *is* a higher Source, a universal consciousness you can tap into. The next eight words, "be you in charge for I will follow," are about alignment. They're about moving into the Present Room and receiving internal guidance from our Divine Source. When we feel that presence inside of us, we can follow its direction and the new script that is being written for us.

The next three words help form one of the most important concepts that anyone can ever master. "Certain your direction" is a knowing that we receive constant guidance, or direction, from a higher Source. It's not a thinking, or a hoping, but a knowing. It's constant because there is never a time that it stops. There are only times when we are unaware of its presence. It's the electricity in the house that stays on even when the lights are turned off. If we know this power exists, we can connect to it in any moment. The last four words, "will give me peace," is the joyous result of surrendering to our Higher Power. It does not imply that our life will be okay, or one specific problem will be resolved, but that we will experience peace. What is peace? It is nothing short of Heaven. When we experience total peace, we experience Heaven on Earth. Twenty-three words to experience Heaven on Earth. Why not give it a try? Read it. Memorize it. Live it.

Ultimately, it's not the words of the mantra you choose that give it power. Anybody can recite a bunch of words without effect. The real power comes from when you contemplate the meaning behind the words of the mantra, which you must feel for yourself. Concepts like surrender, trust, knowing, and peace: These are the things you need to feel for the mantra to be effective for you.

MENTAL STICKERS

When you are on the spiritual path and frequenting the Present Room, all is well. When you leave the Present Room, the trouble begins. The real task for everyone is to keep going back. For that, you need to leave yourself little mental stickers, like sticky notes for the brain, to remind you when you should move back into the Present Room. It's all about remembering where you came from, or as Neale Donald Walsch calls it, "re-membering." Essentially, he is saying that we sometimes forget we are all members of the same consciousness, but when we remember that we are all connected to the same Source, we return to our state of connectedness with the other members. In effect, we re-member with the others.

Here are some little stickers for your memory, to help you re-member with the Present Club:

LET'S GO!

Whenever you're alone and about to go somewhere, get in the habit of saying to your Higher Self, "Let's Go!" This will serve as a reminder that you are never alone and the Divine presence is always with you. That simple act of acknowledgment to your Higher Self brings you into the Present Room, and you can start to watch your play of consciousness as the Present Movie.

MY HIDING PLACE

The musical group Sela sings a beautiful song called "You Are My Hiding Place." They're not talking about a physical place but a place in your mind where you can go to stop the ceaseless chatter that occupies too much of our time. Your hiding place is always accessible. We should all have a place we can instantly go that brings us peace and joy. If you don't have one, find it. Finding your hiding place is the same as finding the Present Room.

JUST SAY HI!

Each morning for more than thirty years, during my commute to New York City I would run into many of the same people. Over the course of one morning, I'd say *hi* to Ali at the Long Island Railroad newspaper stand; to Big John and his father Sean at the coffee cart outside our building; to Faye, the security guard, as I walked through the turnstile to our building; and to Meagan, the receptionist, as I arrived upstairs. Many of us do the same thing every day. We greet all these different people because we feel we know them. It's a simple acknowledgment from one person to another that we recognize them and want to show that we care enough to greet them. That little *hi* acknowledges their presence in our lives.

If we are able to acknowledge strangers whom we run into throughout the course of a day, why don't we do the same to our creator? How often do we acknowledge God's presence? How often do we say *hi* to our Divine Source, to show appreciation and gratitude for everything we have and not bitterness for what we don't have? If we go through each day of our lives greeting other people, many we don't really know, why wouldn't we say *hi* to the creator of all people? Because most of us are not aware of God's presence throughout the day. We're too caught up with what's going on in our lives, so we lose awareness of our connection to the Divine. That's really sad, because a little *hello* to our Higher Self can reconnect us to our Source, and we get a huge burst of energy each time we acknowledge its presence within us.

The more we know our Source, the more we'll keep checking in with it throughout the day and begin to know that Source more deeply. That's the real secret. But don't beat yourself up too much if you realize you're not saying *hi* directly to your Higher Self, because the truth is that whenever you say *hi* to the doorman, or the crossing guard, or the mailman—whenever you say it to anyone during the day—you're saying it to their Higher Self, too, which is the same as saying it to yours.

Now think of how many times you greet people you know really well—friends from work, neighbors, people you have grown up with. These greetings are usually accompanied by a handshake, a hug, or a kiss. You wouldn't consider not saying *hi*. Then there are your immediate family, your children, your significant other. Saying *hi* to them is good, but saying *I love you* is even better. Sometimes, we tell our loved ones that we love them multiple times a day. When I first started dating my wife, after we greeted each other, I'd constantly ask, "Have I told you lately that I love you?" It never failed; she'd always answer no, even if I'd just told her I loved her five minutes earlier. She just loved to hear it, and that was our little game. It was warm and kind, and it put a smile on our faces every time. Needless to say, when we got married, our wedding song was "Have I Told You Lately That I love You?" Debby isn't the only one who likes to hear those three words. We all do. It warms our hearts. So don't be afraid to say *I love you*, but even if you don't say those three words, at least say *hi*.

WELCOME BACK

The meaning of the term *welcome back* is that you are returning to something and being greeted with open arms. It's not "I see that you're back—where the hell have you been?" or "What are you doing back here? I told you I never wanted to see your face again!" When someone says *welcome back* to you, they're expressing their pleasure in seeing you again. Even if there was a past conflict between the two of you, they've let go of any fear-based feeling they may have had. In other words, there is only peace and acceptance in the term *welcome back*.

Every time you acknowledge the Divine presence inside you by saying *hi*, you can hear those same two words: *welcome back*. Every time you step into the Present Room and greet all the spiritual masters, they'll all respond in unison, "Welcome back." If you get pulled into other rooms by our thoughts, our awareness of where we are allows us to move back into the Present Room. At that point, we just say, "Hi," and we'll hear that friendly response, "Welcome back."

PLEASE AND THANK YOU

The words *please* and *thank you* are more than just important words; they are critical pieces of the co-creation process. *Please* signals your intent, but not just any old intent. To plead is to ask for something with a powerful emotion. Yes, we are taught to say *please* to be polite, but when we emphasize the word *please*, or say something like *pretty please with sugar on top*, we are calling forth a greater level of intention, we are pleading, and this strong intention is the beginning of the creative process.

Thank you is our way of expressing gratitude to our Higher Power. Yes, we are taught it is polite to say *thank you* to someone who has done something nice for us, but there are far greater benefits to the words *thank you* than showing you have good manners. Saying *thank you* to your Higher Power is an act of appreciation that allows you to recognize your oneness with that higher consciousness. It is like saying *thank you* to the universe for allowing you to experience Divine love while you are in this physical form. So express gratitude not for what you have but for what you *are*—a human being able to experience Divine love. Showing appreciation and gratitude keeps you on the spiritual path. As Meister Eckhart succinctly put it, "If the only prayer you ever say in your entire life is thank you, it will be enough."[5]

Sometimes we have trouble expressing gratitude because we don't feel we have a lot to be grateful for. We have challenges in our jobs, our health, or our relationships. No matter what the cause, when we'd rather say, "Life stinks" than "Thank you, God, for allowing me to feel your presence," we are watching the wrong movie.

There are always tons of people willing to trade their challenges with those who think their lives stink. But usually, the greater the challenge, the more appreciation for life people show, not less. Dan Millman, in *Way of the Peaceful Warrior: A Book That Changes Lives*, has a spiritual teacher who tells him, "Wake up! If you knew for certain that you had a terminal illness—if you had little time left to live—you would waste precious little of it! Well, I'm telling you, Dan—you do have a terminal illness: it's called birth. You don't have more than a few years left. No one does! So be happy now, without reason—or you will never be at all."[6]

WHAT'S NEXT?

The Law of Attraction impacts our everyday lives. But one of the biggest misperceptions about this law is that it doesn't require any action. It can be misinterpreted as simply thinking about all the money you would like to accumulate, and when you wake up in the morning, there suddenly will be piles of money at the foot of your bed. It works that way figuratively but not literally. From a practical standpoint, if you imagine yourself with more money and allow yourself to feel what it would be like to have that money in your bank account, you can begin the process of receiving inspired ideas that will guide you to take the necessary steps to achieve the financial abundance you imagined. Part of the process, however, is to *act* on those inspired ideas. That's where the phrase "What's next" comes in.

When you constantly ask your Higher Self, "What's next?" you train your mind to be listening for that next sign, or intuition, that will let you know where to go and what to do. You are listening because you stop being the thinker of the thoughts that come from your lower self and instead become the receiver of the thoughts that come from your Higher Self. They both have creative powers, but we must learn to differentiate between the two. We can always tell the difference by how they make us feel. The resistant thoughts from your lower self always originate from the Past or Future Room, and if you follow that script, you will be forcing yourself to do things that don't feel right. This in turn attracts more things into your life that don't feel right. Meanwhile, inspired ideas always feel good and originate from the Present Room. It's your Higher Self guiding you toward the script it has written for your Present Movie. That's the director you want to listen to. So, the Law of Attraction is not without action. It just depends on which room you are in and to whom you direct the question, "What's next?"

RECHARGE YOUR INTERNAL MOBILE DEVICE

I don't know anyone who doesn't have a mobile device—at least, no one older than ten. You can't walk down the street without seeing people glued to their smartphones. In the morning, everyone makes sure their mobile device is charged. People seem to pay more attention to how much power they have left on their mobile device than to how their sick neighbor might be feeling. If your phone dies, you feel as if a part of you will die as well. How will you be able to communicate? Your connection to everyone and everything would be gone!

Now think of the human body. Although we know we are more than our body, it still needs to be recharged too. Do we give it the same attention we give our personal phone? Not even close. We walk out of the house in the morning without checking to see whether it has power. We go through the day and may not even think about recharging it with healthy food. When the red light of our internal mobile device comes on, we tend to ignore it.

Our body gives us warning signs, but often either we're oblivious to them or we disregard them. When our energy drains, we walk around on autopilot. Our spiritual mind-body connection is lost, and we may go the entire day without recharging. Sometimes it takes days before we recharge, sometimes much longer. Maybe it's time to start paying as much attention to the connection between our physical form and our light form as we do to the power in a six-inch mobile device.

How do we recharge the personal mobile device we call our physical body? We can eat healthy, exercise, and get plenty of rest, but we can also raise our vibrations. Spread love. Show forgiveness. Be positive. There are many ways to raise our vibrational frequency, and being negative is not one of them. We all admire positive people, so why do so many of us have so much negativity? Negativity stems from a feeling of fear. Positivity stems from a feeling of love. Every time we are not feeling love, our body is telling us it needs to be recharged. It is telling us that we need to raise our vibrational frequency. It is telling us to step back into the Present Room.

CHAPTER 10

THERE'S REALLY
ONLY ONE ROOM

WE ARE HERE ON EARTH SO THAT WE CAN REALIGN WITH THE Source energy from which we came. The feeling of alignment with our eternal being can be called enlightenment, nirvana, Heaven, or whatever term feels right. But whatever you call it, only in the Present Room can you experience that Divine consciousness by remembering your connection to it.

If your thoughts are in the Past or Future Room, generating negative feelings, they are not in alignment with your Source. They are false mental projections. They are illusions. You simply cannot access Divine consciousness unless you are in the Present Room. When you are in the Past or Future Room, you're really unconscious. You are dreaming. That's why all the mystics throughout the ages have always implored us to wake up. They have urged us to awaken from the dream of illusion. When you wake up, you can only be in the Present Room.

Let's go back to some of the feelings you experience in the Past Room, like anger, jealousy, bitterness, and regret. What do they all have in common? They are all rooted in fear. When your thoughts are stuck in the Past Room, they are dominated by fear. Now let's look at some of the feelings you experience in the Future Room, like stress, anxiety, pessimism, and lack. What do they all have in common? They, too, are all rooted in fear. Finally, let's look at the feelings you experience in the Present Room, like peace, joy, appreciation, and compassion. What do they all have in common? They are all aspects of love. You can't find fear in the Present Room because it cannot coexist with love. There is only love, and only love is real. Therefore, only the Present Room, where you experience love, is real.

The Great Assumptions

There are many great spiritual teachings, but most of them are based on assumptions that aren't always clear to us. That's why they are easier said than done. Here are a few of them:

Spiritual teaching—
"Forgive us our sins as we forgive those who sin against us."

Assumption—
That we have already forgiven those whom we believe have sinned against us.

The Lord's Prayer does not say, "Forgive us, Father, even though we haven't forgiven those who have sinned against us." It clearly states, "Forgive us our sins *as* we forgive those who sin against us." This prayer is repeated millions of times per day, but has everyone who says this prayer already forgiven all those who have ever sinned against them? I would guess no, because we all seem to have our own levels of forgiveness for what people do to us. Yet Christ didn't give us any rating system for what should or should not be forgiven. We've made that up ourselves. We expect God's grace but can't grant a little forgiveness to our neighbor in return. Unfortunately, it doesn't work that way. We will continue to feel as if we're not forgiven for what we've done until we forgive others for what they've done.

Spiritual teaching—
"Love your neighbor as yourself."

Assumption—
That we love ourselves.

You may be thinking, *I do love myself. I just got a nice promotion. I live in a nice apartment in the city. I am dating on a regular basis. I love my life.* Many people claim to love themselves but are not really happy. Why? You need to love "who you are" inside and not "where you are" on the outside. You need to truly love yourself.

Loving yourself is no different from the lesson in forgiveness. We feel the love inside, and that is the greatest love of all. The teaching is not to love your neighbor *before* you love yourself. It is not to love your neighbor *more* than you love yourself but to love your neighbor *as* you love yourself. You start with loving yourself, and then as you feel your vibrational energy rise, you're able to love your neighbor the same way because you recognize they are the same vibrational being you are inside.

Spiritual teaching—
"Love God."

Assumption—
That we know God.

How can we love someone we don't even know? When Socrates taught the importance of knowing thyself, he was really telling us to know that part of ourselves where we are one with our Source. In effect, he said, "Know God." He certainly wasn't telling us to know the needy, fearful, false part of ourselves. He was telling us to know the part of ourselves that is peaceful, loving, and compassionate. That is our true self. That is where we are one with God. Hence, to "know thyself" means to "know God." To know God is to love God, because if you truly know God, you know God is love.

So who is God? Is God a mean entity who judges us at the end of our life? A vengeful God who brings famine and disease to this earth? Or a peaceful, loving God? Is God the sunset, the mountainside, the glaciers? Or is God the ghetto, Times Square, the subway? God is really all of the above. People love sunsets and find God there but hate dirty places and think God can't be there.

People also love diamonds but don't want to touch a piece of coal, never realizing coal is a diamond. It's nice to think of a kind, loving person as having Divine qualities, and you like to see yourself as similar to that person. Well, you are the same on the inside, but how about the not-so-nice person? You don't want to think you have anything in common with them, but you are still the same person! That is not because you are a jerk too but rather because that person may act like a jerk on the outside, but there is pure divinity on their inside—same as yours!

Spiritual teaching—
"Transcend the ego."

Assumption—
We are aware of our ego.

You can't transcend something until you realize it is there, blocking your path. The ego is definitely trying to block your way. It's the guide who is constantly trying to lead you down the wrong path. As it's the loudest voice, it's the one you hear most frequently. After a while, it's the only one you hear. To transcend is to rise above or overcome. To transcend the ego, you have to shut it up. It's as though you've pushed a button and trapped the ego in a soundproof room. It's still there, screaming at you to listen, but you can't hear it. All you can hear in the stillness is the quiet voice of the Holy Spirit.

THE PARADOX OF THE TEACHINGS

Embodying any one of these spiritual teachings is exponentially better than embodying none of them. But you'll feel the maximum impact when you are able to perform them in tandem. Although you may have mastered the art of forgiveness, you aren't guaranteed the peace and joy you've been striving for unless you've mastered the art of loving yourself, as well. We must take ownership of both. We need to love ourselves *and* we need to forgive others. Otherwise, we may find ourselves in a contradictory and unresolved situation, such as: "I keep forgiving that person but I still don't feel good about it." That's because forgiving someone else does not mean allowing yourself to be treated like a punching bag.

Consider those difficult relationships where one partner is physically or verbally abusive, but the other partner so desperately wants the relationship to work that they keep "forgiving" the other person over and over. This pattern keeps repeating itself, leaving the abuser free to continue the abuse without consequences and the forgiver feeling beaten down with no place to go. The forgiver may have mastered the art of forgiveness, but they have not learned to love themselves. When they master both, then at the next sign of abuse, they'll be able to issue an ultimatum, something like: "I forgive you for what you did, but next time it happens you will not be coming back." Or better yet, "I forgive you and I will miss you!" When we truly love ourselves, we stick up for ourselves and can follow through on our pledge with the same conviction as if the abuser were trying to hurt our child. It's the child in us that we're protecting. Be fierce in protecting that child.

THE PARADOX OF CHANGE

We're always trying to get other people to change, to be like us and see the world the way we see it. We make assumptions about the world, which translate into our beliefs, and then we try to get the people in our lives to believe what we believe. But what if our beliefs and assumptions are wrong? In that case, getting people to change won't help anyone. Furthermore, while it has been said that the one constant in our everyday lives is change, many people are petrified of change. They try to prevent it or just plain ignore it, but there it is anyway—change, change, change. In actuality, change happens in the physical world, and we can't prevent or stop it. We need to realize the eternal being inside of us never changes. But we *can* change the way change affects us.

Wayne Dyer liked to tell the story of when the great saint Swami Muktananda in India was asked, "What is real?" He replied, "What is real is that which never changes."[1] But aren't we all part of the cycle of change? Everything is evolving and changing all the time. The rain comes down and then evaporates back into the sky; plants grow and then are eaten by animals; animals die and then return to feed the earth, which grows new plants. The physical world constantly changes—but does that mean none of it is real? No. In fact, Muktananda's statement, "What is real is that which never changes," is true—but the opposite is also true. As the Buddha states, "Everything changes, nothing remains without change."[2] Both these observations are true; as Herman Hesse states in his enlightening book *Siddhartha*, "The opposite of every truth is just as true."[3]

So instead of thinking, "I am changeless," we should recognize that we are part of that which is always changing. Nature doesn't need to do anything to change. It just changes on its own. A chrysalis turns from a moth to a butterfly all by itself, driven by the innate power of its being. We are part of that evolution. We are part of everything that ever was, that keeps evolving, that is now, and that ever will be.

THE PARADOX OF SEPARATION

We need to create separation in order to understand there is no separation. *A Course in Miracles* speaks of the Atonement, which is the realization that our separation from God never occurred. One of the deepest truths we should strive to grasp is that we have never separated from our Source. Yet to experience oneness with our Higher Self, we have to separate from our lower self. We need to recognize that we are not that person consumed with fearful thoughts. In other words, we need to create separation from our ego in order to see there is no separation from the Holy Spirit.

In the Past Room, our thoughts are driven by fear and the belief that we are separate from everyone else. In the Future Room, our thoughts are driven by fear and the belief that we are separate from everyone else. In the Present Room, our thoughts are driven by love and the knowledge that we are made of the same substance as everyone else. There is only one of us here, and we are all it. If everyone moved into the Present Room at the same time, the world would simply be as one.

FREE WILL

Who doesn't like free will? It's as though the heavens have given us the right to do whatever we want. I could be a police officer but then decide to switch and become a sanitation worker instead. I might know I shouldn't eat that second piece of cake for dessert but choose to eat it anyway. I may add a few extra pounds on my waist, but that's my right. Free will. *Can you believe what that jerk did to me? He's going to pay for that. I am never forgiving him. That's my right.* Powerful stuff, this free will. It gives us the power to make choices, and we think there are an unlimited number of choices. In reality, there is only one choice: to remember our connection to our Source or to forget it. We are the only creatures in our universe who get to make that choice.

Hence, our need for free will. If we choose to remember our connection to our Source, we will be blessed with the positive emotions of the Present Room. If we choose not to remember, our belief in separation from each other will continue to saddle us with negative emotions. That is our choice. That is our free will.

You always have the choice of which room to hang out in and which movie theater to sit in. That is your Divine right. You can choose to live in the present or choose not to. You can choose the Holy Spirit or you can choose the ego. When you remember your connection to your Source, you have chosen the Present Room. Ironically, once you choose the Present Room, free will no longer applies to you. It's not that someone has taken it away; you just don't need it. When you get lost while driving, you hit "go home" on the navigation system. Once you're finally sitting in your driveway, you still have a button on your navigation system that says "go home," and it's a tremendous function, but you don't need it because you're already home.

On this planet, we've all been granted the power of free will to remember our Source or not. If we choose to remember, we produce positive energy and live in peace and harmony. If we choose to forget, we produce negative energy and experience the consequences. Either way, there is no interference from our Source. That is the one condition of free will.

INTERCONNECTIVITY

One of the most useful skills we learn in life is how to tap into the power of connection. As people say, "It's not *what* you know but *who* you know." We are always trying to network so that we can make connections with people we think can help us get ahead. However, forcing the universe in this way doesn't work. For example, you want to meet the influential designer Brian in order to show him some of your designs. So you go to a party because Sam will be there, and Sam's sister is best friends with Jodi, Brian's cousin. You figure if you meet Sam, maybe you'll get to know his sister, who can introduce you to Jodi. Now you'll know Brian's cousin. You haven't figured out how you will actually get to Brian yet, but if you do, you can work your magic to try to get something out of him.

The likelihood of making a strong connection with Brian under those circumstances is very remote because you are trying to force it to happen. Instead, if you declare your intention internally that you would like your designs to be seen by the right people, your inner being immediately starts writing the script for you to meet all the people necessary for you to achieve your desire. That script is ready for you to watch in the Present Theater. Meanwhile, a different script is playing out in the Future Theater because you are trying to figure out all the right connections and worrying about if it will happen. In the Present Theater, you allow your Higher Self to do it for you, and you expect it to happen.

Too often, we put much more emphasis on making connections in the external world than in our own internal world. We believe successful people can open a few doors for us so we can achieve the goals we desire. But if you remembered your connection to your Source, you'd have a connection that would unlock not just a few doors but *any* door.

You are not only connected to Divine consciousness; you *are* it. So is everyone else. We are all connected. This concept is at the heart of all spirituality. The part of us that is connected is the part of us that is real. These connected parts of each of us are attracted to each other based on what we feel, and our emotions determine what is real for us. As Wayne Teasdale says, "The reality of any being is related to its interconnection with all other beings or entities."[4]

THE DISCONNECT

For centuries, mystics, sages, and saints have chosen to stop speaking with others in their daily lives in order to reach a deeper level of contemplation. They sought to communicate internally with their Higher Power by disconnecting from the everyday chatter about worries, regrets, deadlines, and commitments. These teachers understood that when you disconnect with the general public on the outside, you are more readily able to reconnect with your Source on the inside. This isn't really a disconnect, however, because you realize we are not separate beings but are all connected at a cosmic level.

Today, technology is shutting us off from each other. Instead of sitting around and talking, groups of friends all over the country are sitting around ignoring each other and texting. Just look around and you'll see evidence of it everywhere.

One Memorial Day, my family went to the beach on a beautiful sunny day, and the first thing I saw was a group of teenagers hanging out, not saying a word to each other . . . but all texting or staring at their phones. Later that day, I took my daughter, then six years old, to the pool. When she jumped off the diving board, I looked up at the lifeguard. To my surprise, he was sitting with his arms tucked inside his T-shirt, so it looked like he was wearing a straitjacket. When I looked closer, I saw that his hands were popped out at the bottom of his shirt. He was holding a cell phone, looking down and texting away. When my daughter climbed out of the pool and ran back to the diving board, this young man, who was charged with saving her life if she started to drown, was totally oblivious to the young girl right in front of him jumping into twelve feet of water.

Where is this trend leading us? The irony is that the internet is the greatest communication system ever created to connect people, but it ends up disconnecting us. The real question is: Do you use the internet to bring you closer to other people, or do you use it as a vehicle to push people away? Do you use it to help others or to avoid others? When enough people use the amazing power of the internet to spread news that makes our creator smile, then we will start to see real change in the world.

Throughout history, most generations have spent much of their time alone with their thoughts. The ancient Greeks didn't have televisions. The Romans didn't have smartphones. Even Abraham Lincoln had to read books by candlelight at night. People in the past were forced to spend a lot of time alone, either connecting with their Source or connecting with their interpretations of what other people say and do. With few people around, there was more time to spend alone and less resistance to accessing the Divine. The French philosopher Blaise Pascal must have been pleased that past generations were forced to sit alone in a room.

Today, so many people spend most of their time on their smartphones using apps and social media. How are they supposed to understand the concept of Divine consciousness, let alone experience it? The internet is the greatest resource for spreading awareness of Divine consciousness we've ever had. Christ traveled on foot, as did the Buddha. Today, it is possible for one person to have millions of Twitter followers. But if that is their connection to the world we see, the world of form, what is their connection to the world we don't see, the invisible world of light? Hopefully, it is just as strong.

Digital communication is not the problem in and of itself; it's the fact that the communication stems from the same thoughts as in the world of form. People are still hanging out in the Past Room, and they can text a hundred people to tell them what someone else did. Even worse, some people tell lies and spread false accusations online with the sole intent of harming each other. Rather than disconnecting to look within and see the situation from a clearer, more peaceful perspective, they use technology to attack.

People become more vicious when they have the ability to be anonymous. It's easier to be nasty when you're not looking at or speaking directly to someone. Online vicious communication can be relentless, even if there are only two people involved.

Disconnecting from your daily life does not mean sitting alone in front of a flat screen or looking at a mobile phone. It means turning away from electronic devices and reconnecting to your Higher Self. Once you've moved back into the Present Room, you could use the mobile device to uplift other people, not to tear them down. But until you put down your electronic device, you will never get back to the Present Room and reconnect to your Source.

RELATIONSHIPS

People tend to make judgments based on first appearances, but mobile devices have taken judging someone based on how they look to a new level. Look no further than the explosive growth in online dating apps that let you view a stream of pictures. Are these effective dating tools? That's debatable.

You need to recognize such apps for what they are—entertainment. The real challenge comes when some users treat it like a game and are only interested in the way that their dates look, but others take it very seriously and are interested in developing relationships. Now you have a disconnect. Any time we place all our attention on physical appearance, or the world of form, we lose contact with our internal appearance, or the world of light.

It is the same as only seeing people through the external mirror. Recognizing someone for who they are inside takes much more time and effort.

If you look back at the World War II and Korean War generations, couples tended to enter into relationships at a young age and stay in them through thick and thin. They went through an extended learning process, during which they could work through their problems and grow even closer as time went on. A long courtship period typically allowed them to discover what they were each like inside. It was not unusual for couples of this generation to celebrate wedding anniversaries fifty or sixty years later.

Still, that does not mean everyone lived happily ever after. Some couples stayed in unhappy or unfulfilling relationships because one or both of them were afraid of expressing exactly how they felt as they grew older, even though their values and interests may have changed. On the outside, they looked like a happy couple, but on the inside, one of them may have felt trapped. Their children, the Baby Boomers, were less reluctant to express their feelings. Divorce rates rose as people began to feel that they shouldn't have to stay in a relationship if they were not happy. Is that better? On one hand, they may not have felt as trapped, but on the other hand they may have given up on a relationship before it had a chance to develop fully. They could still be searching for their soul mates when, in fact, they walked away from them many years before.

Many people talk about wanting to meet their soul mate but don't take the time to learn what the person they are dating is all about. Too often we judge and then dismiss a person before ever getting close to their soul. There is a better way. The first night I met my wife, we both felt something special inside. Our knees touched while we sat facing each other in the Tribeca Grand lounge in New York, and neither of us moved our knees. We felt a physical connection on the outside that touched something on the inside, and it felt right. Within five months we were engaged. But before that happened, while we were really getting to know each other, I sent her a copy of *The Invitation* by Oriah. It was plain to see that Deb was beautiful on the outside, but I needed to know what moved her on the inside. *The Invitation* is a powerful story that implores us to look at the strength and beauty within our partner, rather than their age, appearance, or occupation.

The only way to discover a real connection with another human being is to feel it inside. When you and your partner both feel the love that connects us inside, you're in for something wonderful. If you want a great partner, don't spend too much time looking, judging, and criticizing the outside package. That is not who anyone is. That's not what will sustain the relationship when times get tough—and they *will* get tough. No matter who you are or what your life is like right now, you will experience trying times in your life. In those times especially, you will want to look at life through the eyes of our creator, seeing the beauty within all things, and to have a partner who will do the same.

YOUR ENERGY SOURCE

As humans, we are creators of energy, and our physical bodies are storage facilities for those energies. It's up to us which type of energy we create. The Present Room is filled with love, joy, and compassion. Whenever we are centered in the Present Room, we create positive energy. It invigorates us, drives the feeling of love and joy into every inch of our being, and puts a little extra zip in our step.

It seems hard to believe anyone would want to feel anything else—but we do. When our thoughts are focused in the Past or Future Room, we can generate feelings that are byproducts of fear. This produces negative energy, which we store in our bodies. This negative energy, whether conscious or subconscious, puts a tremendous strain on our bodies. In effect, it drains our positive energy.

STOP GENERATING NEGATIVITY

Once you experience how easy it is to generate negative thoughts, you begin to see how easy it is for others to generate negative thoughts as well. These thoughts are not just imaginary, they are forms of energy, and because we are all connected at a vibrational level, they can be distributed among us. For instance, suppose someone you know is having a bad day and gives you a nasty look or says something mean to you. Instead of acknowledging that insult and letting it go, you could internalize it. You have stored their negative energy inside yourself, and you may even pass it on to someone else. The negative thoughts can not only affect our emotions but also have a damaging effect on someone else's. Conversely, positive thoughts and emotions produce positive energy. When we send that energy out into the world, it can have a profound impact on the world we see.

The same remarkable change can happen to your internal energy levels. You can fill up with more energy than you ever thought possible. When you hang out in the Past and Future

Rooms, your energy continues to drain and you don't even realize it. But when you move into the Present Room, the spiritual energy stored in the Present moment will immediately restore you to the point where you feel as energized as you've ever been. Then something truly miraculous happens. By remaining in the Present Room, you continue to fill with this beautiful energy *beyond* the point you thought possible. Your heart begins to expand, and your capacity to love continues to grow. Before you know it, you are fully connected to the Divine consciousness, or the Divine matrix, that connects every particle of the universe. You become one with everything and everyone, and the power of love that you experience in every moment is beyond anything you ever dreamed possible. That's where you want to be. That's what you want to experience. And you can, at any time—except, of course, when you don't.

When negative energy gets trapped in your body, it doesn't want to let go. You'll then go through all kinds of avoidance strategies so those negative energies won't bother you. You convince yourself that you've "overcome" them and go merrily on with your life—until, out of nowhere, they rear their ugly heads again. Someone pushes that button, which "re-minds" you of the event that first produced that negative energy, and you experience it all over again.

Suppressing negative energy is not the same as getting rid of it. You must release it, and the only way to do that is to feel it again and then forgive it. You must go back to the beginning and identify the root cause of the negative energy. Then forgive him, her, or yourself. If the anger stems from a trapped memory of something someone did to you, you need to forgive the other person. If it's guilt over something you did, you need to forgive yourself. Nobody can do that for you. You are the only person who will ever know if you've truly forgiven yourself or others. If you haven't, you'll continue to harbor negative energy. If you have, you will be free.

The perfect illustration for this concept literally fell into my lap. As I was writing this morning, my eight-year-old daughter came and sat on my lap. She asked what I was writing about, so I read her the previous paragraph on negative energy getting trapped in our bodies. Then I stopped. "Let me explain this a different way," I said.

"Let's suppose you go to school on Monday and one of the boys in your class—let's call him Tommy Smith—puts ice cream in your hair during lunch period. It's messy and gross. All the kids laugh at you and you feel really humiliated. Even Tommy is laughing and pointing at your hair. This really bothers you, and it takes a few days for you to get over it. Even though other kids stop teasing you, for the rest of the school year, you don't speak to Tommy. You're too mad at him. At the beginning of the next school year, Tommy moves out of town, and you never go to school with him again. Forward twenty years, and you see Tommy at a party in New York City. One of two scenarios can play out:

"Scenario One: As soon as you see Tommy, you remember the anger and humiliation you felt when he put the ice cream in your hair. You tell your friends, 'I can't believe that jerk Tommy Smith is here.' When he comes up to say hello, you shout, 'You've got some nerve, Tommy! Don't even try to talk to me after what you did!' You storm away and end up making your friends leave the party.

"Scenario Two: At some point later in your life, you think of the ice cream incident with Tommy and how it made you feel. You allow yourself to get mad at Tommy again, and then you let it go. You forgive Tommy, because he was just an eight-year-old boy who didn't know any better. So when you see him at the party twenty years later, you smile about the incident in elementary school. When he comes up to talk, you say, 'Hi Tommy, how are you? Do you remember when you smeared ice cream in my hair? I was so mad at you back then. Now, I look back and that was pretty funny.' The two of you share a laugh and catch up on your current lives.

"So, Rebecca, which one of these two scenarios would you rather experience?"

"That's easy, Dad. I'd pick scenario number two," she replied.

"Very good, sweetheart, but you know what's really funny? Most grown-ups seem to choose scenario number one."

"That doesn't make any sense, Dad."

She's right. It doesn't make any sense. Why is it that an eight-year-old can recognize the importance of releasing stored negative energy from our bodies, but most adults can't seem to do this? We'd rather suppress those negative emotions for twenty years and then let them explode on an unsuspecting adult. Go figure.

The only way to start restoring your positive energy is to stop draining it. The only way to stop draining your energy is to stop focusing on things that bothered you in the past or on things you don't want to happen in the future. The only way to stop draining your energy is to move out of the Past or Future Room. Then, and only then, can you start to replenish your energy in the Present Room.

Being in the Present Room means there is only a connection to the greatest Source of energy in the universe. As you are being filled with this energy, your capacity to hold this energy, your capacity to love, will expand. As your heart expands, your focus shifts to feelings of gratitude for allowing you to feel this way, which turns up the dial to allow your heart to expand even further. This is when people say things like, "He's on a roll." It means you are keeping your focus on the connection to Divine consciousness and that connection to your Source has filled you with positive energy. The Source knows no limits. You fill with more spiritual energy, or love, which expands your capacity to love, which generates more feelings of gratitude, and on it goes. You are now on a roll, or in a positive feedback loop. In other words, you are in the Present Room, and you will never want to leave.

EXTRAORDINARY ENERGY

As I noted earlier, the marrying of science and religion becomes more apparent every day. Quantum physics is now saying that we are all made of the same substance because we are all connected to one unifying Source energy that connects all the cosmos. As Max Planck, who won the Nobel Prize in Physics in 1918, once said, "All matter originates and exists only by virtue of a force which brings the particle of an atom to vibration and holds this most minute solar system of the atom together. We must assume behind this force, the existence of a conscious and intelligent mind. This mind is the matrix of all matter."[5]

While this may be hard to grasp, we can either go on doubting or we can go out and find answers. Lynne McTaggart is a renowned author who went on a personal quest to find scientific evidence to prove that our consciousness is an energy that can actually affect physical matter. She is a journalist, not a scientist, but she came to realize that Newtonian science, which has served as the definitive explanation of the universe since the 1700s, describes the inanimate world we see, or Big Matter, as a collection of interconnected energy particles. But this theory was not extended to include living things. Instead, we have traditionally been viewed as a collection of separate, disconnected beings. This didn't make sense to McTaggart. So with the help of renowned quantum physicists like Dr. Fritz-Albert Popp, she set out to show that we are all connected the same way Big Matter is connected. Her investigative work led her to write a number of books on intention, consciousness, and energy. Her 2002 book, *The Field*, is a powerful affirmation that not only are we humans all connected by a unifying field of energy, as Max Planck expressed, but that our consciousness can also physically affect the matter we see and feel every day.[6]

It seems to follow from her research that when our heart consciousness teams up with this field of energy, we can defy the laws of physics as we know them. We have all seen examples of the inexplicable. Sometimes we call them miracles. My friend Angelo's parents owned a pizza place in town called Jack's Pizzeria. When I was around twelve, I used to work there with Angelo. One day, Angelo and I were there working when we heard a loud crash. We ran outside. There, right in front of us, was a car smashed into a telephone pole, with Angelo's mother trapped underneath the front left wheel. Before we could fully take in what had happened, we saw Angelo's older brother Steve lifting the front corner of the car all by himself, until he'd lifted the wheel completely off his mother.

As we watched in stunned silence, someone else yelled, "Quick, get her out!" A few people who'd come running over dragged Angelo's mother out from under the car. Steve then dropped it with a thundering boom. Soon an ambulance arrived to take care of his mother. Angelo and I kept standing there staring at Steve as if he were from another planet. Even he couldn't fully comprehend the magnitude of what he'd just done. A seventeen-year-old boy could never singlehandedly pick a car up into the air and hold it there, and yet he had.

So how was Steve able to defy the laws of physics? Intent and emotion. When he saw his mother trapped under the car, he had one intention—to save her. He didn't question whether he was strong enough or the car weighed too much. Subconsciously, he imagined himself lifting that car, and powerful emotions coursed through his body. The love he felt for his mother was profound. Clearly the combination of intent and heart emotions can overcome the laws of physics.

There are countless stories of people like Steve defying all odds to save someone in an emergency. They mixed intent with heart emotion and altered the physical laws in the universe. There is no other explanation. You can call it adrenaline, but where does adrenaline come from? It comes from inside us. Since it appears that people can defy the laws of physics in an emergency, why can't we do it when we are *not* in an emergency? A crisis simply removes the doubt and raises the emotions. But if we can find a way to do that, we don't need a crisis.

Awakening from the Dream

Hopefully by this point in the book, the following has new meaning for you.

"We are all sleepwalking. Most of us just don't know it yet."

It's clear that we can never awaken if we believe we are separate from everyone else. But, believing we are connected to everyone else is not enough to awaken us. We may understand that we all share a common connection to our Source, but we need to actually *experience* our oneness with the Divine consciousness we all share before we can *know* it to be true.

We are responsible for how we experience life. We experience it by feeling it. You are the only person who knows what you feel. If you feel only love for everything you see, then you have experienced the Present Room. This allowing of love to direct your life experience is your true awakening.

The concept of awakening from the dream is one of the hardest to grasp. That's what all the mystics have implored us to do for centuries, and if it were easy, they wouldn't have had to stress it so much. If it were easy, we'd all be awake already. The real question is, how do you know when you have awakened? Is something magically different, something that you'll recognize right away? When you awaken from the dream, something must be different from when you were in the dream, otherwise you'd never know you were awake.

The difference is in how you feel. Once you have awakened, you'll have an appreciation for all things. You'll feel compassion for all people. You'll notice an absence of fear and an overwhelming feeling of peace. You won't use labels; you won't judge. When you finally awaken, you will see yourself in everyone and everything, and it will be good.

To awaken from the dream is to simply remember who you are: an eternal being sharing a human experience with other eternal beings. When you remember that, then you become an eternal being who is aware of your human experience. Once you are aware of your human experience, you can watch the Present Movie from your seat of consciousness. You can't be aware of your oneness with all other eternal beings if your thoughts are stuck in the fear-based Past or Future Room.

That is why there is only *one* room, the Present Room. This room is your connection to your Source and love. When you watch your human experience from the Present Room, you realize that your awareness is real and the play is the dream. When you watch from that place, you have awoken.

Simple? Yes. Easy? No. Our biggest challenge in getting to that place is that we think our minds can clearly see the world, and if someone says we need to wake up, our first reaction is to say, "What the hell are you talking about? I'm already awake." The person sleepwalking is thinking, "I am wide awake and I can see everything. I can see this tree and I can see that person." They even determine the difference between right and wrong, who is good and who is bad.

When you're sleepwalking, what you feel is determined by what you see in the world. When you are awake, what you see is determined by what you feel. The person who is awake is think-ing, "I am wide awake and I am everything. I am this tree and I am that person." They walk around and see themselves in everything. They have no concept of good or bad; the world just is. When you are sleepwalking, you look around and say, "I see this, and I see that." When you are awake, you look around and say, "I am this, and I am that."

EPILOGUE

IT WAS EARLY MAY, AND I WAS MEETING MY FRIEND LARRY Glenz at my house for an hour to catch up before he went to coach lacrosse practice down the block. I arrived late and Larry was already there, sitting in his car, holding a book. I apologized as soon as I left my car. He said it was no problem; it gave him time to finish the book he was reading.

"Actually, you should read this book," he said. "You'd enjoy it. It is written by a guy named J. D. Messinger, who is a distinguished graduate of the United States Naval Academy and a successful businessman. He had a near-death experience, and he writes here about an internal dialogue he had with his Higher Power."

"Sounds a lot like the Neale Donald Walsch book *Conversations with God*," I said.[1]

"Yes. Very similar concept."

I took the book and tossed it on the coffee table before we

headed out to the backyard. We talked, and I told Larry about an experience I'd had one night several months earlier. I'd been standing looking at myself in the bathroom mirror when I'd felt moved to ask my reflection, "Who am I?" A very clear internal voice answered, "I am you."

I told Larry that I'd immediately known the voice wasn't coming from my ego but from my Higher Self. It was also clear that the message was not directed just to me but to everyone. In those three words, my Higher Self was telling me, "I am you, I am him, I am her, I am everyone." We are all connected to the same higher consciousness, and that is who we really are. We are not the body we're looking at in the mirror.

I told Larry I'd started writing a book and that was going to be one of its main themes.

Soon, Larry left for lacrosse practice. I went in, picked up the book on the coffee table, and read the title: *11 Days in May*. I turned to the table of contents, which listed a series of incredibly interesting questions Messinger was asking his Higher Self. But I was immediately drawn to the last chapter, "Who are you?"

This was virtually the same question I'd asked my Higher Self only months before, and I was really intrigued to see what answer Messinger had come to. I turned to the last chapter and this is what I read:

JDM—
I have one more question for you.

HS—
What is that? I thought I answered everything already.

JDM—
Who are you?

HS—
That's a silly question. I am you.[2]

I felt chills go down my spine. *What are the chances?* It was amazing to think that I would read this message at this moment, that I happened to be late, which gave Larry extra time to finish the book, that Larry happened to offer me the book to read. How amazing that I then decided to tell Larry about my experience with the bathroom mirror, and that when he left, I picked up the book and found Messinger asking basically the same question to his Higher Self that I'd asked my reflection, "Who are you?—and most amazing of all—for me to have received the exact same answer.

On second thought, I suppose the *least* surprising of all in this chain of events is that he and I both got the same message. We are constantly creating the world we see, whether we realize it or not, so encounters and events are always popping up in the physical world after we've thought about them in our minds. When this takes us by surprise, we call it a coincidence. When we expect it to happen, we call it synchronicity.

The message, for me and Messinger, was clear, and it was no coincidence. There are many paths but only one truth, and that truth is that we all share the same Divine consciousness. I am you. You are me. We are one.

Acknowledgments

TO THE TEAM AT GREENLEAF BOOK GROUP, THANK YOU FOR turning this vision into a physical reality. April Murphy, my lead editor; Sarah Hudgens, my copy editor; Jen Glynn, project manager; Danny Sandoval, consultant; Brian Phillips, cover design; Corrin Foster, branding and marketing; Olivia McCoy, marketing associate; I am blessed to work with such a talented and delightful group.

To Nancy Doherty, my first editor, thank you for trusting in me and for your thoughtful insights and direction.

To Lynn Serafinn, for your guidance in explaining the message of *The Three Rooms*. And to your talented daughter, Vrinda Pendred, for editing and proofing.

To Renee Duran, for your brilliant cover and web design.

To my publicist, Jackie Lapin, thank you for guiding me in sharing the message of *The Three Rooms*.

To my parents, for your lifelong commitment to your children. I hope you are smiling on us from heaven.

To my siblings, Ray, Greg, and Doreen, for helping to teach me about sharing and caring for one another.

To all my family and friends, thank you for your constant support.

To my coach, friend, and mentor Larry Glenz. We have shared an incredible spiritual journey, you and me. We knew that remarkable things were going to happen in our lives long before they began to manifest in the physical world.

To my lifelong friend Gregg Lorberbaum. You have always been there for me through all of life's trials and tribulations. If I ever had a true life coach—it was you.

To my children, Brendan, Paul, and Rebecca. You have been my greatest blessings on this earth. I watch in wonder as you continue to discover that divine light within you.

Finally *to Deb, the love of my life*. You have always loved me for who I am inside. You can see things in me that nobody else can. Whenever my thoughts leave the Present Room, you are the first person to recognize it and remind me to go back home. I am forever grateful for you.

Chapter Notes

Introduction

1. Eckhart Tolle, *A New Earth*. New York: Penguin Group, 2006, p259.
2. Wayne Teasdale, *The Mystic Heart*. California: New World Library, 2001, p11.
3. Henry David Thoreau, *A Week on the Concord and Merrimack Rivers*. Originally published in 1849. Retrieved from *The Observer*, article by John Summers, April 20, 2010.
4. Al-Anon slogan: "Take what you like and leave the rest." Retrieved October 30, 2017 from http://www.alanon .activeboard.com/t58308228/take-what-you-like-and-leave -the-rest/.

CHAPTER 1

1. Albert Einstein, "Science, Philosophy and Religion, A Symposium." New York: the Conference on Science, Philosophy and Religion in Their Relation to the Democratic Way of Life, Inc., 1941.
2. Thich Nhat Hanh, *Living Buddha, Living Christ*. New York: Penguin Publishing Group, 1997.
3. The Holy Bible Old and New Testaments, *King James Version*. Proverbs 23:7. New Zealand: The Floating Press, 2008.
4. Helen Schucman, *A Course in Miracles*. T-3.111.6, 4-5. Mill Valley, California: Foundation for Inner Peace, 1975.
5. His Holiness the Dalai Lama, "Dalai Lama XIV Quotes." Goodreads. Retrieved October 27, 2017. https://www .goodreads.com/author/quotes/570218.Dalai_Lama_XIV.
6. The Holy Bible Old and New Testaments, *King James Version*. Matthew 7:1-3. New Zealand: The Floating Press, 2008.
7. Martin Handford, *Where's Waldo?* New York: Little, Brown and Company, 1987.
8. Dr. Viktor Frankl, *Man's Search For Meaning*. Boston: Beacon Press, 1959.
9. Paul Bryant, "Laura Moncur's Motivational Quotations." The Quotations Page. Retrieved October 27, 2017. http://www.quotationspage.com/quote/39900.html.

CHAPTER 2

1. John C. Maxwell, "John C. Maxwell Quotes." BrainyQuote. Retrieved October 30, 2017. https://www.brainy quote .com/quotes/quotes/j/johncmaxw451128.html.

2. The Holy Bible Old and New Testaments, *King James Version*. Luke 23:34. New Zealand: The Floating Press, 2008.

3. Helen Schucman, *A Course in Miracles*. Mill Valley, California: Foundation for Inner Peace, 1975.

4. Richard Carlson, *Don't Sweat The Small Stuff . . . and It's All Small Stuff.* New York: Hyperion, 1997.

5. *Forrest Gump.* Directed by Robert Zemeckis. Los Angeles: Paramount Pictures, 1994.

6. *Big Hero 6.* Directed by Don Hall and Chris Williams. Burbank, California: Walt Disney Animation Studios, 2014.

7. Neville Goddard, *The Power of Awareness.* Seattle: Pacific Publishing Studio, 2010, p77.

8. *Good Will Hunting.* Directed by Gus Van Sant. Los Angeles: Miramax Films, 1997.

9. Eckhart Tolle, "Bad Memories? Eckhart Tolle's Advice on How to Deal." Huffington Post, December 12, 2012 edition. https://www.huffingtonpost.com/2012/12/12/bad-memories-eckhart-tolle-how-to-deal_n_2260002.html.

CHAPTER 3

1. Dr. Joe Dispenza, *You Are the Placebo.* Carlsbad: Hay House, 2014, p98.

2. *Spider Man.* Directed by Sam Raimi. Culver City, California: Columbia Pictures, 2002.

3. Gabrielle Bernstein, *Spirit Junkie: A Radical Road to Discovering Self-Love and Miracles.* UK: Hay House, 2011.

4. Daniel Chidiac, *WHO SAYS YOU CAN'T? YOU DO.* Australia: DC Group Global, 2012, p338.

5. *The Hunger Games*. Directed by Gary Ross. Santa Monica, California: Lionsgate, 2012.

6. Bobby McFerrin, "Don't Worry Be Happy." Simple Pleasures. EMI-Manhattan Records, 1988, compact disc.

7. Bob Marley, "Three Little Birds." Exodus. Polygram Records, 1977, compact disc.

8. Jon Mundy, *Perfect Happiness*. New York: Sterling Publishing Co., Inc., 2014.

9. Linda Ellis, 1996. *The Dash Poem*. 1996–2017 Copyright Inspire Kindness, LLC.

10. *Gladiator*. Directed by Ridley Scott. Universal City, California: Dreamworks Pictures, 2000.

11. Wayne Teasdale, *The Mystic Heart*. California: New World Library, 2001, p.219.

12. Abraham Maslow, "Abraham H. Maslow Quotable Quotes." Goodreads. Retrieved November 1, 2017. https://www .goodreads.com/quotes/290951-a-musician-must-make -music-an-artist-must-paint-an.

13. Abraham Maslow, *A Theory of Human Motivation*. Originally Published in *Psychological Review*, 1943. 50, 370–396.

14. Henry Ford, "Henry Ford Quotable Quotes." Goodreads. Retrieved November 1, 2017. https://www.goodreads.com /quotes/978-whether-you-think-you-can-or-you-think-you -can-t--you-re.

15. Wayne Dyer, "Wayne Dyer Quotable Quotes." Goodreads. Retrieved November 1, 2017. https://www.goodreads.com /quotes/649413-banish-doubt-when-doubt-is-banished -abundance-flourishes-and-anything.

16. *Glory Road*. Directed by James Gartner. Burbank, California: Walt Disney Pictures, 2006.

17. The World Health Organisation statistics. Retrieved November 1, 2017. https://www.befrienders.org /suicide-statistics.

CHAPTER 4

1. Alexander Pope, "Alexander Pope Quotable Quotes." Goodreads. Retrieved November 1, 2017. https:// www.goodreads.com/quotes/19218-to-err-is-human -to-forgive-divine.

2. Iyanla Vanzant, *In the Meantime*. New York: Simon and Schuster, 1999.

3. The Holy Bible Old and New Testaments, *King James Version*. Luke 17:21. New Zealand: The Floating Press, 2008.

4. Jules Verne, *Journey to the Center of the Earth*. France: Pierre-Jules Hetzel, 1864.

5. *Cocoon*. Directed by Ron Howard. Los Angeles: Twentieth Century Fox, 1985.

6. Bob Dylan, "Blowin' in the Wind." The Freewheelin' Bob Dylan. Sony,1963, compact disc.

7. Katy Perry, "Firework." Teenage Dream: The Complete Confection. Capitol, 2012, compact disc.

8. *Ghost*. Directed by Jerry Zucker. Hollywood: Paramount Pictures, 1990.

9. Anita Moorjani, *Dying To Be Me*. Carlsbad, California: Hay House, Inc. 2012.

CHAPTER 5

1. John Lennon, "Beautiful Boy." Double Fantasy. Capitol, 2000, compact disc.

2. *The American President*. Directed by Rob Reiner. Culver City, California: Columbia Pictures, 1995.

3. Winston Churchill, "Winston Churchill Quotable Quotes." Goodreads. Retrieved November 2, 2017. https://www.goodreads.com/quotes/16489-never-give-in-never-give-in-never-never-never-never-in.

4. Eckhart Tolle, *The Power of Now*. Vancouver: Namaste Publishing, 1997.

5. June Steenkamp, Taken from interview with Savannah Guthrie on Today, March 4, 2014. Retrieved on November 2, 2017. https://www.today.com/news/reeva-steenkamps-mother-i-can-forgive-oscar-pistorius-2D79315362.

6. *Frozen*. Directed by Jennifer Lee and Chris Buck. Burbank, California: Walt Disney Animation Studios, 2013.

7. Abraham Maslow, "Abraham H. Maslow Quotable Quotes." Goodreads. Retrieved November 2, 2017. https://www.goodreads.com/quotes/560514-be-independent-of-the-good-opinion-of-other-people.

8. Michael Strahan. *Wake Up Happy: The Dream Big, Win Big Guide to Transforming Your Life*. New York: Simon & Schuster, 2015.

CHAPTER 6

1. *The Matrix*. Directed by Lana Wachowski and Lilly Wachowski. Burbank, California: Warner Bros. Pictures, 1999.

2. Michael Singer, *The Untethered Soul: The Journey Beyond Yourself.* Oakland: New Harbinger Publications, 2007.

3. Wayne Teasdale, *The Mystic Heart.* California: New World Library, 2001. p167.

CHAPTER 7

1. Patricia Cota Robles, *ASCENDING INTO YOUR I AM PRESENCE*, June 14, 2014. Retrieved on November 3, 2017. https://www.eraofpeace.org/news /ASENDING-INTO-YOUR-I-AM-PRESENCE/.

2. Emmet Fox, I am . . . it is your true being . . .

3. Neville Goddard, *The Power of Awareness.* Seattle: Pacific Publishing Studio, 2010. p10.

4. *A Knight's Tale.* Directed by Brian Helgeland. Culver City, California: Columbia Pictures, 2001.

5. Shonda Rhimes, "Shonda Rhimes '91, Commencement Address." Dartmouth College Commencement, Dartmouth. June 8, 2014. http://www.dartmouth.edu/~commence /news/speeches/2014/rhimes-address.html.

6. Abraham Lincoln, "Abe Lincoln Quotable Quotes." Goodreads. Retrieved November 3, 2017. https://www .goodreads.com/quotes/9938-whatever-you-are-be-a-good -one.

7. *Heal.* Directed by Kelly Noonan. Beverly Hills: Elevative Entertainment, 2017.

8. The Holy Bible Old and New Testaments, *King James Version.* Samuel 16.7. New Zealand: The Floating Press, 2008.

9. *Friday Night Lights.* Directed by Peter Berg. Beverly Hills: Imagine Entertainment, 2004.

10. The Holy Bible Old and New Testaments, *King James Version*. John 14.20. New Zealand: The Floating Press, 2008.

CHAPTER 8

1. Meister Eckhart, *Breakthrough: Meister Eckhart's Creation Spirituality in New Translation*. Translation by Matthew Fox. New York: Doubleday, 1980, p141.
2. "The Parable of the Mexican Fisherman." Renewable Wealth. http://renewablewealth.com/the -parable-of-the-mexican-fisherman/.
3. *Sliding Doors*. Directed by Peter Howitt. London: Intermedia, 1998.
4. The Holy Bible Old and New Testaments, *King James Version*. Luke 15:11–32. New Zealand: The Floating Press, 2008.

CHAPTER 9

1. Michael Acton Smith and Alex Tew, *Calm*, application for phone. 2015.
2. Raul Julia, *Raul Julia Quotes*. Retrieved on November 3, 2017. http://www.famous-quotes.cc/authors/raul-julia /quotes/84940.
3. Helen Schucman, *A Course in Miracles*. Mill Valley, California: Foundation for Inner Peace, 1975.
4. Ibid., Lesson 365.

5. Meister Eckhart, "Meister Eckhart Quotable Quotes." Goodreads. Retrieved November 3, 2017. https://www.goodreads.com/quotes/644785-if-the-only-prayer-you-ever-say-in-your-entire.

6. Dan Millman, *Way of the Peaceful Warrior: A Book That Changes Lives*. California: HJ Kramer, 1980.

CHAPTER 10

1. Wayne Dyer, "Why Settle for Ordinary?" *Heal Your Life*, February 4, 2013. https://www.healyourlife.com/why-settle-for-ordinary.

2. Buddha, "Buddha Quotes." Thinkexist. Retrieved November 3, 2017. http://thinkexist.com/quotation/everything_changes-nothing_remains_without_change/147320.html.

3. Hermann Hesse, *Siddhartha*. New York: New Directions Publishing, 1951, p143.

4. Wayne Teasdale, *The Mystic Heart*. California: New World Library, 2001, p219.

5. Max Planck, "Max Planck Quotable Quotes." Goodreads. Retrieved November 3, 2017. https://www.goodreads.com/quotes/1328821-all-matter-originates-and-exists-only-by-virtue-of-a.

6. Lynn McTaggart, *The Field*. New York: HarperCollins, 2008.

Epilogue

1. Neale Donald Walsch, *Conversations with God, Book 1.* Newburyport: Hampton Roads Publishing, 1995.
2. J.D. Messinger, *11 Days in May.* California: Waterside Publishing, 2012.

AUTHOR Q&A

1. *What is the most important lesson or takeaway you want read-ers to get from reading your book?*

    We all have control over how we feel. Our thoughts have the biggest effect on our emotions; it's just we're not very good at monitoring them. The conscious awareness of our thoughts in any moment allows us to focus on pleasant-feeling thoughts rather than thoughts that produce negative emotions. When we learn how to monitor our thoughts, we get better at con-trolling our emotions. When we learn how to control our emotions, we change our experience of life.

2. *What would you suggest to someone who is having trouble being in the present despite your advice already written here?*

    Most people understand how important it is to monitor our thoughts, but we just don't. Sometimes our thoughts are moving too quickly, so I would tell someone to begin with identifying how they feel. Based on how you feel, you can start to recognize which room your thoughts are in. Once you are consciously aware of which room your thoughts are in, you can intentionally begin the process of moving back to the Present Room.

3. *Who has inspired you to be a better, more mindful person?*
We have much to learn from the spiritual masters throughout history. They taught us to listen to our "inner teacher" more than what we learn from others. This inner teacher is the first voice I try to listen to every morning. But we also have amazing modern-day teachers. Wayne Dyer and Neville Goddard both inspired me to be more mindful. Marianne Williamson, Eckhart Tolle, and Abraham-Hicks have also had a big influence on my life. Still, our greatest teachers are all the quiet ones who demonstrate love every day in their lives. Those people are all around us.

4. *What interaction in your life has had the most influence on you?*
The most challenging times in my life have had the most influence on me because they are the moments that forced me to look inside myself for answers.

5. *Did you discover anything new about yourself while writing this book?*
Yes. I discovered more than ever that true self-confidence doesn't just come from your accomplishments or feedback

from other people. It comes from truly liking the person you
see in the mirror.

6. *What was the most difficult aspect of writing this book?*
I had to learn to write what I felt compelled to say and not
what I thought people wanted to hear.

7. *Do you really consider yourself a mystic?*
I consider everyone a mystic-in-training—myself included.
Some people may say that not everyone can be a mystic, but
I don't believe that. Mystics don't have anything that others
don't have. They just don't have a lot of the negative thinking
that others have to contend with. I think you also need to
agree on what a mystic is. To me, a mystic is someone who
devotes their life to knowing God and who understands that
we are all eternal beings, connected to Source energy, who
have manifested in physical bodies. In addition, a mystic is
one who has aligned vibrationally with their eternal being.
I know that I have had mystical experiences. I strive to have
more of those moments.

8. *Where do you "see" God in your daily life?*
What we see is just our perception. Before you can see God
in your life, you have to feel God in your life. Once you feel
that part of you that is connected to our Source, which is
your Higher Self, then you can allow that part of you to see
through your eyes. Now you start to see your life from the
perspective of your Higher Self. That becomes your new perception of reality. That means you are watching the movie of
your life from the Present Theater.

9. *What is next for you?*

    I have begun writing a second book that expands on many of
    the principles of *The Three Rooms*. It is a fictional book called
    The Land of Perception and Time.

10. *You speak of having your own day of reckoning like Lieutenant
    Dan from Forrest Gump. Looking back, would you change any-
    thing that led to that moment for you?*

    I wouldn't want to change anything that has happened in
    my life. That is not to say that everything in my life has gone
    the way I thought it would, but we tend to want to keep the
    "good" things that have happened to us and get rid of the
    "bad." But this tendency comes from just making judgments,
    and many times, what we believe to be good we later deter-
    mine to be bad, and what we label as bad we later determine
    to be good. In reality, there is no good or bad, just our per-
    ception of it.

11. *What do you feel is the biggest obstacle to our ability to remain
    in the present?*

    Our thoughts are our biggest hindrance to remaining in the
    present. We don't need to monitor our thoughts so we can get
    back to the Present Room; we need to monitor our thoughts
    to keep them from pulling us out.

12. *You mentioned how Generation Z is also beginning to feel the
    impact of stress. How early should the mindfulness you speak of
    be practiced?*

    Our children are never too young to be mindful of their
    thoughts and, therefore, their emotions.

13. *How would children and young adults get started on a mindful way of life in the present?*

The best way for children to learn about mindfulness is to make it a game. The more fun you have with monitoring your thoughts, the better at it you will become. Since all children like to play games, you can play "Which room are my thoughts in?" Also, if you see someone exhibiting negative behavior, you can ask your child, "Which room are they in?" The better they get at identifying which room someone else is in, the better they will be at recognizing which room their own thoughts are in.

14. *Is this the responsibility of their parents? Teachers? Other adults? Or is this something they need to come to on their own?*

We are all responsible for teaching mindfulness to children. But we teach by demonstrating. If you are not practicing it yourself, then you certainly can't teach it to children. So our number one responsibility is to align with our own Higher Self in the Present Room first. Then we can teach our children how to do the same.

15. *What inspired you to write this book?*

I was always curious as to why some people appeared so happy when it seemed they had so little, and others appeared so unhappy when it seemed they had so much. I started asking a lot of questions, internally, to better understand. The answers didn't come right away, but one day the whole concept of the Three Rooms came all at once.

16. *You use many movie references throughout this book to explain your musings. Do you think that viewing a film can be a spiritual experience?*

    Absolutely. I love movie references because there are so many inspiring movies that produce the feelings of compassion and appreciation that bring us back into the Present Room. I also love to watch movies based on true stories. We are all participating in our own life movie, and when we watch a biography, we get to see how someone's thoughts and emotions directly impact what manifests in that character's life.

17. *Do you find yourself struggling to stay in the Present Room even today?*

    Of course I do. Ironically, *The Three Rooms* is all about how your thoughts affect your experience of life, but I don't focus on my thoughts to tell me which room I am in. I focus on how I feel. Your thoughts can fool you, but your emotions never lie. If I feel good, I constantly show appreciation for everything in my life. Even the little things. This helps keep me in the Present Room. If I start feeling negative emotions, I know my thoughts are not aligned with the thoughts of my Higher Self. Do I move instantly back into the Present Room? No. But it is easier to get back there when you know you have left.

18. *How do you personally break the bad habits that put you in the Past and Future Rooms?*

    This process starts with understanding where your thoughts come from. If we focus on what we see and hear all around

us, with everyone's differing opinions, then we start to produce the resistant thoughts that put us in the Past or Future
Rooms. However, when we focus on how our inner being
feels in any situation, we are no longer affected by what others say and do. The resistant thoughts that put us in the Past
or Future Room are replaced by thoughts we receive from
our Higher Self in the form of inspired ideas. Those inspired
ideas will help keep us in the Present Room.

READERS GUIDE QUESTIONS

1. Based on how you feel, which room do you think you spend most of your time in?
2. Can you name three people you know who spend the majority of their time in the Past Room? (Hint: anger, guilt, shame)
3. Can you name three people you know who spend the majority of their time in the Future Room? (Hint: stress, anxiety, fear)
4. Can you name three people you know who spend the majority of their time in the Present Room? (Hint: joy, appreciation, love)
5. What are some of the times you've been stuck in the Past or Future Rooms?
6. Would you agree that your soul, or your Higher Self, is always waiting for you in the Present Room?

7. What do you do to keep yourself in the Present Room?

8. What has been the most helpful/inspiring takeaway from reading this book?

9. How has reading this book changed the way you perceive others? Has it changed the way you judge others/react to situations? Explain.

10. Do you "see" God as outside of you or as inside of you? Discuss.

11. What changes to your daily life will you make after reading this book?

12. Discuss situations when you helped others realize that they are enough. What did you do to make them feel that way? What can you do in the future to lead others to that realization?

13. Has anyone made you to feel that you are not enough? What did you do to overcome that feeling?

14. How often do you meditate? As thoughts come up, can you recognize which room they are in?

15. Discuss where you are on your journey to mindfulness. Are you a beginner? Can you recognize when your thoughts pull you out of the Present Room?

16. The author mentions many spiritual leaders and their philosophies. Who are some spiritual leaders who have had an impact on you?

17. What are some things that you felt brought you joy and happiness before reading this book? What do you feel brings you happiness after reading it?

18. The author points out that the younger generations of Millenials and Generation Z are feeling the effects of stress and

anxiety more than any before them. What are some ways you can and will help those of a younger generation that you interact with to feel less stress and allow them to affect a present mindfulness?

19. Love is a major theme the author discusses. What is the importance of love in guiding yourself to present mindfulness?

20. The author discusses many films as sources for his spiritual journey. What are some of your favorite movie scenes that lead you to be a more mindful person?

About the Author

KEVIN MURPHY IS A FORMER WALL STREET MANAGING DIREC-
tor, high school and collegiate wrestling champion, community
activist, speaker, coach, and debut author of the book *The Three
Rooms*.

During his highly successful thirty-three-year career at Citigroup, Kevin was responsible for the sales, marketing, and trading of several different businesses within the firm. He served on
the Board of Directors of multiple option exchanges and spoke
at conferences all over the world. He is a former chairman of the
SIFMA Option Committee and has lectured both U.S. Regula-
tory and Congressional staff on the education of the options and
securities markets.

Following his college wrestling career, he has served as a

youth wrestling coach on Long Island for over 30 years. His life-time service to the sport of wrestling led to his induction into the National Wrestling Hall of Fame in 2009. He is a member of the Board of Directors for the non-profit Friends of Long Island Wrestling, and has spear-headed a campaign to raise awareness of the opioid and drug epidemic that is sweeping the country.

These experiences have given Kevin a unique and eclectic mix of understanding human nature. He noticed that our happiness and unhappiness in life is always the result of our thoughts—whether observations of the present, memories from the past, or projected fears about the future. Combining this theory with the deep personal insights he attained along his own twenty year spiritual journey, Kevin uses the metaphor of the Three Rooms to explain how observing which room your thoughts are in, can change your experience of life.